CASAS TEST PREP STUDENT BOOK

FOR

READING GOALS FORM 907R/908R

LEVEL D

Preparing Adult Learners for CASAS
Reading GOALS Tests and for Workforce
and College Reading

By Coaching for Better Learning, LLC

CASAS TEST PREP
STUDENT BOOK FOR READING GOALS
FORMS 907R/908R LEVEL D

Preparing Adult Learners
for CASAS Reading GOALS Tests
&
Workforce and College Reading

COACHING FOR BETTER LEARNING

COACHING FOR BETTER LEARNING

TABLE OF CONTENTS

INTRODUCTION

This test prep student book is designed to successfully develop adult learners' academic reading skills, preparing them for CASAS Reading GOALS Level C Forms 907R/908R tests and vocational training, admission reading tests. In other words, this student textbook presents academic reading activities that help adult education programs and workforce programs and their learners meet the Workforce Innovation and Opportunity Act (WIOA) reading expectations.

The reading exercises and answer keys of this test prep student book cover CASAS Reading GOALS Level C standards and College and Career Readiness (CCR) reading standards and content. For example, each lesson focuses on three main areas: ***vocabulary, reading comprehension skills and higher-order reading skills.***

The reading passages presented are from various sources—journal articles, newspaper clippings and nonfiction and fiction books—and cover a wide range of topics. You will have the chance to reflect on what you have learned as you complete practice tests at the end of the lessons.

READING STRATEGIES

This student reading textbook covers and teaches the following reading strategies:

- *Effective Vocabulary Strategies*
- *Using Your Background Knowledge*
- *Topic vs. Main Idea: What's the difference?*
- *Learning to Summarize*
- *Drawing Inferences*
- *Comprehension Monitoring*
- *Question-Answer Relationships*
- *The Importance of Text Structure*
- *Figuring out Figurative Language*
- *Examining the Point of View*
- *Analyzing the Author's Purpose and Technique*
- *Evaluating the Credibility of Texts*

The textbook is designed for adult learners as an instructional guide for the development of reading comprehension skills. It offers academic reading strategies to help adult learners become more active, strategic and purposeful readers. The use of these strategies will also help learners understand and remember what they read.

Reading is an active and thinking process. Therefore, this book encourages learners to actively engage with texts by predicting, making connections and inferences, asking and answering questions, and completing the comprehension activities.

This textbook provides practice exercises for using the reading strategies to access different types of texts (science, social studies, technical texts and literary texts). The lessons emphasize text complexity, evidence and knowledge.

All the reading strategies are presented with examples, pictures and text. These learning aids will help you understand the strategy and how it works, as well as give you hands-on practice. As you read, study and work through these examples, you will build the confidence to succeed. **You will become a strategic reader**. Let's get started!

Before we move on, let's start you off by filling in the box below:

WHAT DO I KNOW ABOUT READING COMPREHENSION?	WHAT DO I WANT TO KNOW?

LESSON 1
VOCABULARY STRATEGIES

By the end of this lesson, you will be able to utilize strategies to determine the meaning of unknown words.

While reading, it is common to encounter words that you don't know. These words can be any of the following:

- Technical words
- Domain-specific words
- Multiple-meaning words

Thankfully, there are clues that you can use to understand unknown words and phrases. These clues are called **context clues**. Let's have a look at the types of context clues you can use.

1. DEFINITION OR EXPLANATION CLUES

Sometimes, writers explain the meanings of difficult words in texts. They may give these definitions or explanations in the same sentence as the word or in the following sentences.

Example: _Orthoses, devices placed on the body to guide and assist movement, help in the healing process of the affected body part._

In this example, the word "orthoses" is explained to the reader within the same sentence: "devices placed on the body to guide and assist movement."

PRACTICE EXERCISE 1

Circle the meaning of the underlined word in the sentence below.

A main physiological cause of hypocapnia is rapid breathing. Symptoms of this reduction in carbon dioxide in the blood include abnormal heartbeats, tingling sensations and muscle cramps.

a. An infection of the lungs
b. A decrease of carbon dioxide in the blood

c. An increase of carbon dioxide in the blood
d. Muscle contractions throughout the body

2. EXAMPLE CLUES

In some cases, writers use examples that can help you figure out the meanings of unknown words. Look out for words and phrases that signal examples are being given: "for example," "including," "such as" and "like."

Example: _The Greater London Built-up Area is the largest conurbation in the United Kingdom, as it includes urban towns such as London, Surrey and Berkshire._

In the example, we learn that the meaning of "conurbation" is an urban area that consists of several towns. We know this as we get examples of the urban towns that it includes.

PRACTICE EXERCISE 2

Circle the meaning of the underlined word in the sentence below.

As a _cosmologist_, Dr. Khan's job deals with the solar system, stars and galaxies.

a. A person who studies elements of the earth.

b. A person who provides cosmetic treatments.

c. A person who searches for aliens.

d. A person who studies the entire universe.

3. SYNONYM CLUES

Synonyms are words that have similar meanings. Sometimes, an unknown word would have a synonym in the passage that you **do** know. In this way, you can figure out the unfamiliar word.

Example: *When Mandy looked in the fridge, there was a variety of _comestibles_. However, she wasn't interested in any of the _foods_ available.*

The meaning of the word "comestibles" is revealed in the synonym clue, "foods."

PRACTICE EXERCISE 3

Circle the meaning of the underlined word in the sentence below.

Luis was not only _enamored_ by the magnificent architecture, but the natural scenery also bewitched him.

a. To have strong feelings of admiration

b. To protect oneself with armor

c. To be fascinated by nature

d. To have strong feelings of disgust

4. ANTONYM CLUES

Antonyms are words that are opposite in meaning. The text you're reading may have an antonym for the unknown word that would help you figure out its meaning.

Example: *The witness offered _trivial_ information on the suspect when we needed more _important_ details.*

The type of information that was given was "trivial." However, "important" information was needed. We can tell that "trivial" is the opposite of "important." Therefore, the word means "unimportant."

PRACTICE EXERCISE 4

Circle the meaning of the underlined word in the sentence below.

Mr. Chanka _amassed_ a fortune during his lifetime. However, everything was promptly spent by his son after he died.

a. To allocate

b. To scatter

c. To gather

d. To consume

PRACTICE EXERCISES

Excerpt 1

Read the following excerpt.

> *The mechanical properties of wood are its fitness and ability to resist applied or <u>external forces</u>. By external force is meant any force outside of a given piece of material which tends to deform it in any manner.*

What is the meaning of the phrase "external forces?"

a. Types of woods that are very resistant

b. The internal features of wood

c. Weak pressure from outside sources

d. Pressure from outside sources that change materials in some way.

Excerpt 2

Read the following excerpt.

> *Warmth is also <u>conducive</u> to the growth of fungi, the most favorable temperature being about 90°F. They cannot grow in extreme cold, although no degree of cold such as occurs naturally will kill them.*

Which meaning is the same as "conducive," as it is used in the excerpt?

a. To have a high temperature

b. To be advantageous

c. To be useless

d. To have a low temperature

Clue: _

Excerpt 3

Read the sentence below.

> *Metals and glass expand equally in all directions, since they are <u>homogeneous</u> substances, while wood is a complicated structure.*

1. Which word can best replace "homogeneous" without changing the meaning of the sentence?

a. Different

b. Complex

c. Disorganized

d. Alike

2. What type of context clue does the writer provide?

a. Synonym clue

b. Antonym clue

c. Explanation clue

d. Definition clue

Excerpts from *The Mechanical Properties of Wood* by Samuel J. Record

REFLECTION ON LEARNING

Answer the following reflection questions and feel free to discuss your responses with your teacher or a classmate.

- What reading idea or strategy did you learn from this section?

- What new concepts did you learn?

- What methods did you work on in this section?

- What aspect of this section is still not 100 percent clear for you?

- What do you want your teacher to know?

LESSON 2
USING YOUR BACKGROUND KNOWLEDGE

By the end of this lesson, you will be able to use your background knowledge to understand and connect with texts.

When you activate your **background** or **prior knowledge**, you connect your knowledge and experiences with the text you're reading. This skill helps to make the text more meaningful and relatable to you. There are **three** types of connections you can make.

1. TEXT-TO-SELF

In this type of connection, you use your **personal experiences** and **emotions** to understand the text you're reading.

Example: When reading a passage about national parks, you remember the times that you've visited national parks, as well as your observations and feelings during the visits.

TEXT-TO-SELF
Connect with the text you're reading using your personal experiences.

Ask yourself:
"How does this text remind me of my own life and experiences?"

2. TEXT-TO-TEXT

Using this type of connection, you connect the text you're reading with other texts such as stories, passages and other books by the same writer.

Example: You're reading a passage about John Brown and think, "Oh, I read a passage on Harpers Ferry last week!" You are then able to build, question and change the knowledge you already have.

12

TEXT-TO-SELF
Connect the text you're reading with a book or story you've read before.

Ask yourself:
"Have I read something on this topic before?"

3. TEXT-TO-WORLD

As an adult, you would have gained general knowledge about the world through various mediums such as television, radio, the Internet and interactions with others. Use the knowledge you have gained to understand and connect with the texts you read.

Example: You're reading a passage on the sinking of the Titanic ship. You have never been on a ship or read about a topic like this before. However, your general knowledge would help you understand how the Titanic sunk, as you would already know that boats and ships sink when flooded with water.

TEXT-TO-SELF
Connect the text with the knowledge you have of how the world works.

Ask yourself:
"How does this text relate to the world?"

PRACTICE EXERCISES

Read the passage below and answer the questions that follow. Compare your answers with your partner's.

Buck's first day on the Dyea beach was like a nightmare. Every hour was filled with shock and surprise. He had been suddenly jerked from the heart of civilization and flung into the heart of things primordial. No lazy, sun-kissed life was this, with nothing to do but loaf and be bored. Here was neither peace, nor rest, nor a moment's safety. All was confusion and action, and every moment life and limb were in peril. There was imperative need to be constantly alert; for these dogs and men were not town dogs and men. They were savages, all of them, who knew no law but the law of club and fang.

He had never seen dogs fight as these wolfish creatures fought, and his first experience taught him an unforgettable lesson. It is true, it was a vicarious experience, else he would not have lived to profit by it. Curly was the victim. They were camped near the log store, where she, in her friendly way, made advances to a husky dog the size of a full-grown wolf, though not half so large as she. There was no warning, only a leap in like a flash, a metallic clip of teeth, a leap out equally swift, and Curly's face was ripped open from eye to jaw.

————

An excerpt from *The Call of the Wild* by Jack London

TEXT-TO-SELF	TEXT-TO-TEXT	TEXT-TO-WORLD
Does the text remind you of a personal experience?	Does the passage remind you of any other text you've read?	To what world events does the text relate?
Is the text different from your life?	Is the text different from texts that you've read?	Are the events in the passage different from events that happen in the world?

REFLECTION ON LEARNING

Answer the following reflection questions and feel free to discuss your responses with your teacher or a classmate.

- What reading idea or strategy did you learn from this section?

- What new concepts did you learn?

- What methods did you work on in this section?

- What aspect of this section is still not 100 percent clear for you?

- What do you want your teacher to know?

LESSON 3

TOPIC VS. MAIN IDEA: WHAT IS THE DIFFERENCE?

By the end of this lesson, you will be able to differentiate between the **topic** and the **main idea** of a text.

First, read the passage below.

> 'Numerous innovations and inventors laid the groundwork for the telephone. Samuel Morse's telegraph, patented in 1837, used electric signals to transfer coded messages. In 1840, Charles Grafton Page used electrified wire connected to a magnet to produce sound. In the next decades, Johann Philipp Reis and Antonio Meucci developed electromagnetic devices that could transmit music and some voice communication. But it was a teacher interested in sound and speech instruction for the deaf, Alexander Graham Bell, who would combine the power of electromagnetism with a machinery of vibration and thereby establish the basis of modern telephone technology.
>
> On March 7, 1876, Bell became the first inventor to receive a US patent for the technology that powered the telephone. Working with his assistant, Thomas Watson, Bell initially had a different goal in mind: to develop a "harmonic telegraph" that could send a number of messages at the same time, each at its own pitch. But after an accidental discovery, in which Watson electrified a vibrating reed on the telegraph, Bell and Watson created a device using vibration to produce and receive sound waves through electrical signals. In June 1876, Bell traveled to the Philadelphia Centennial Exposition (the first World's Fair in the United States) to demonstrate this device to an international audience.'
>
> ──────
> An excerpt from 'The Invention of the Telephone' by Franky Abbott

THE TOPIC

The **topic** is a word or phrase that describes the **general** content of the text you're reading. A **precise topic** narrows down the subject matter and **specifically** states what the text is relating.

Look for clues from the title and accompanying images. If they are not available, look for repeated words, related words and phrases, as well as pronouns referring back to the same words.

THE PRECISE TOPIC

Ask yourself:
"What is the passage mainly about?"

Example: The passage given doesn't have a title or accompanying image. However, it clearly discusses telephones. It also describes devices that preceded the telephone such as the "telegraph" and "electromagnetic devices." Therefore, we can conclude that the passage is about "telephones" and more precisely, "the invention of the telephone."

THE MAIN IDEA

When you have identified the topic, you can find the **main idea**. This is the **key point** that the writer wants you to know about the topic. Sometimes, the main idea is **explicit**. Therefore, it is stated in the paragraph, typically in the first sentence. This sentence is called the **topic sentence**.

THE MAIN IDEA

Ask yourself:
"What does the writer want me to know about the topic?"

Example: In the passage given, the first sentence tells you the main idea: "Numerous innovations and inventors laid the groundwork for the telephone."

THE SUPPORTING SENTENCES

The supporting sentences develop the main idea by giving **definitions, explanations, examples** or **reasons**. They answer the following questions: Who? What? Where? When? Why? How?

There are two types of supporting details. **Major supporting details** give more information to help you understand the main idea. The **minor supporting details** give further information about the major details.

Example:

Topic: The Invention of the Telephone

Main Idea: Numerous innovations and inventors laid the groundwork for the telephone.

Major Supporting Details

1. Samuel Morse's telegraph used electric signals to transfer coded message.

2. Charles Grafton Page used electrified wire connected to a magnet to produce sound.

3. Johann Philipp Reis and Antonio Meucci developed electromagnetic devices that could transmit music and voice communication.

4. Alexander Graham Bell combined these inventions to create the telephone.

Let's look at another example.

> On January 24, 1848, carpenter James Marshall discovered gold at Sutter's Mill, a sawmill on the American River in Coloma, California. This news quickly spread across the country and around the world, igniting the California Gold Rush. Between 1848 and 1855, 300,000 fortune-seekers came to California, transforming its population, landscape, and economy. The largest wave of migrants—about 90,000 people—arrived in 1849, earning them the nickname "forty-niners."
>
> In 1848, the US had just taken California from Mexico as a result of the Mexican-American War, and the region's population consisted primarily of Native Americans and people of Spanish or Mexican descent. Gold seekers arrived by both sea and overland routes across the West like the California Trail. As people flooded into mining camps, "boomtowns," and the city of San Francisco, the Gold Rush brought together Europeans, South Americans, Chinese immigrants, and Americans from all walks of life. The tremendous influx of people, paired with open contempt for Native American claims to their ancestral land, resulted in devastating losses for California's Native American population. Gambling, violence, and vigilante groups were common as local government and law enforcement were often nonexistent or ill-equipped to deal with the flood of new arrivals.
>
> ─────
> An excerpt from 'California Gold Rush' by Samantha Gibson

FIND THE PRECISE TOPIC

Remember the steps in finding the precise topic.

1. Read the title and look for images. In this case, there are none.

2. Look for repeated words, related words and phrases, as well as pronouns referring back to the same words.

   Examples:

   "Gold seekers arrived…"
   "…people flooded into mining camps…"
   "…the Gold Rush brought together [people] from all walks of life"
   "The tremendous influx of people…"
   " …the flood of new arrivals"

3. Ask yourself: "What is the passage mostly about?"
   Answer: The influx of people during the Gold Rush

FIND THE MAIN IDEA

Check if the main idea is stated in the paragraph. If it is not, then it is **implicit** or unstated. Look at the **major supporting sentences** and try to figure out what they are describing.

Ask yourself: "What does the writer want me to know about the topic?"

EXAMPLE:

> **Topic:** The influx of people during the Gold Rush

Major Supporting Details	Minor Supporting Details
1. James Marshall discovered gold in California.	1. The US had just taken California from Mexico.
2. People of different nationalities arrived at gold mine camps.	2. California mostly consisted of Native Americans and people of Mexican descent.
3. The Native Americans experienced losses due to the influx of people.	3. Gold seekers arrived by both sea and overland routes.
4. There was rampant lawlessness as a result.	

> **Main Idea:** The influx of people during the Gold Rush had adverse effects in California.

THE MAIN IDEA

Ask yourself:

"Does each major detail support my main idea?"

PRACTICE EXERCISES

Passage 1

The American whaling industry has its roots in the seventeenth century, in small coastal villages on Long Island, New York and Nantucket, Massachusetts, where right whales were so plentiful that they could be caught close to shore and brought back to port for processing. At the height of the whaling industry, however, in the early nineteenth century, large ships would travel the globe for two to three years at a time, killing whales and processing them on board before returning home to sell resulting products. Most important was whale oil, the preferred fuel for lighting American homes prior to gas and electric lighting; it was derived from a whale's blubber or, in the case of a high-quality sperm-whale oil, from a whale's head. Flexible baleen from the jaws of whales was also used to make the bones of women's corsets and a number of other household items. Sailors often passed the time aboard ship by carving designs into whale teeth and bone, an art form known as scrimshaw.

The whaling industry fueled the growth of many New England cities, including Fall River, New Bedford, and Salem in Massachusetts. Crews aboard whaling ships and staff on the docks of whaling ports were remarkably diverse, employing a large number of free African Americans, including Frederick Douglass after he escaped from slavery. Ships would often supplement their crews as they traveled throughout the world; Herman Melville's Moby Dick features crew members from the South Pacific, for example. A young Japanese man named John Manjiro eventually rose to the position of first mate on an American whaling vessel and became the United States' first prominent Japanese immigrant.

_____

An excerpt from 'The American Whaling Industry' by Kerry Dune

1. Circle the precise topic of the passage.

a. Whaling

b. The height of the American whaling industry

c. Significant persons of the American whaling industry

d. American whaling vessels

2. What is the main idea?

a. The crew members of the American whaling industry were diverse.

b. Whale oil was essential in the early nineteenth century.

c. The diverse sailors of the American whaling industry traveled around the world in the early nineteenth century.

d. The American whaling industry was beneficial to cities and persons of diverse backgrounds.

3. Which of the following is a major supporting sentence in the passage?

a. The whaling industry fueled the growth of many New England cities.

b. Large ships would travel the globe for two to three years at a time.

c. Sailors often passed the time aboard ships by carving designs into whale teeth and bone.

d. Crews aboard whaling ships and staff on the docks of whaling ports were remarkably diverse.

Passage 2

In the nineteenth century, in an era known as the Second Great Awakening, philanthropic and charitable efforts grew across the United States. Part of this humanitarian effort focused on educating disabled people. Construction of boarding schools and institutions for deaf and blind students slowly spread across the country and children once considered uneducable now received formal instruction. Nevertheless, the education of deaf and blind people was controversial. Many questioned the influences of public and private funding on the schools as well as the practice of committing children to an institution at a young age, which meant removing them from their families. Varying teaching strategies for deaf and blind children were also debated.

Rev. Thomas H. Gallaudet, Laurent Clerc, and Dr. Mason Fitch Cogswell were influential figures in the growth of instruction for deaf people in North America. In 1814, Gallaudet became interested in this topic after meeting Alice Cogswell, the deaf daughter of his neighbor, Dr. Cogswell. Gallaudet traveled to Europe, where he learned from Abbé Sicard, head of the Institution Nationale des Sourds-Muets à Paris, a famous school for deaf children in Paris. Gallaudet began working at that Institution with Laurent Clerc, a graduate of the school and teacher there. Clerc and Gallaudet then traveled back to the United States, and in April of 1817, Gallaudet, Clerc, and Dr. Cogswell founded The Connecticut Asylum for the Education and Instruction of Deaf and Dumb Persons (later the American School for the Deaf) in Hartford, Connecticut. Gallaudet became principal and Clerc a head teacher at the Asylum.

———

An excerpt from 'Nineteenth-Century Schools' for the Deaf and Blind by Melissa Jacobs

1. What is the precise topic of the passage?

a. The growth of education for the disabled in North America

c. Strategies for educating the disabled

b. The origin of the American School for the Deaf

d. The disabled in North America

2. Which of the following states the main idea?

a. There are various strategies for educating the disabled.

c. In the nineteenth century, formal instruction for the disabled grew in North America.

b. The Second Great Awakening occurred in the nineteenth century in America.

d. There were many important people that influenced instruction for the disabled.

3. Circle the minor supporting sentence below.

a. Construction of boarding schools and institutions for deaf and blind students spread across the country.

c. Rev. Thomas H. Gallaudet, Laurent Clerc, and Dr. Mason Fitch Cogswell were influential figures in the growth of instruction for deaf people.

b. Varying teaching strategies for deaf and blind children were debated.

d. In the nineteenth century, philanthropic and charitable efforts grew across the United States.

REFLECTION ON LEARNING

Answer the following reflection questions and feel free to discuss your responses with your teacher or a classmate.

- What reading idea or strategy did you learn from this section?

- What new concepts did you learn?

- What methods did you work on in this section?

- What aspect of this section is still not 100 percent clear for you?

- What do you want your teacher to know?

LESSON 4

LEARNING TO SUMMARIZE

By the end of this lesson, you will learn to apply strategies to summarize reading passages.

A summary is a short, precise description of a text. To summarize, you must be able to **understand a text**, identify its **key points** and **rephrase** information in your own words.

The following are useful steps you can take to summarize a passage successfully.

1. **Read** the passage and underline or highlight **key words** and **details**.

> **Edgar's father**, a son of General David Poe, the American revolutionary patriot and friend of Lafayette, had married **Mrs. Hopkins**, an English actress, and, the match meeting with parental disapproval, had himself taken to the stage as a profession. Notwithstanding Mrs. Poe's beauty and talent the young couple had a sorry **struggle** for existence. When Edgar, at the **age of two years**, was **orphaned**, the family was in the utmost **destitution**. Apparently the future poet was to be cast upon the world homeless and friendless. But fate decreed that a few glimmers of sunshine were to illumine his life, for the little fellow was **adopted by John Allan**, a wealthy merchant of Richmond, Va. A brother and sister, the remaining children, were cared for by others.
>
> In his new home Edgar found all the **luxury** and advantages **money** could provide. He was petted, spoiled and shown off to strangers. In **Mrs. Allan** he found all the affection a childless wife could bestow. Mr. Allan took much **pride** in the captivating, precocious lad. At the age of five the boy recited, with fine effect, passages of English poetry to the visitors at the Allan house.
>
> An excerpt from *The Works of Edgar Allan Poe* by Edgar Allan Poe

2. Find and write the **precise topic**.

    Precise Topic: Edgar's early life

3. Identify approximately **three major** and **minor** supporting details.

MAJOR SUPPORTING DETAILS	MINOR SUPPORTING DETAILS
• Edgar was orphaned at the age of two.	• Edgar's father was a son of General David Poe.
• He was adopted by Mr. and Mrs. Allan, a wealthy couple.	• Edgar's father's marriage to Mrs. Hopkins was disapproved by his parents.
• He was adored by the couple and had access to luxuries and wealth.	• Edgar's siblings were cared for by others.

4. Determine the **main idea**.

Main Idea: After he was orphaned, Mr. and Mrs. Allan adopted Edgar and treated him very well.

5. **Summarize** the text.

Write the summary by combining all the information that you have. Include the topic sentence or the main idea, as well as one or two major supporting details in your own words.

Summary: After he was orphaned at the age of two, Edgar was adopted by Mr. and Mrs. Allan, a wealthy couple that provided him with many luxuries.

Edgar Allan Poe, Writer and Poet

PRACTICE EXERCISES

Read the passages below and answer the questions that follow.

Passage 1

In 1900, the federal census recorded just over 200,000 American Indian people living in the United States. Most lived on reservations—parcels of land that Indian people had retained in treaty negotiations—over which the federal government claimed jurisdiction. By 1900, the policy of the federal government was that American Indian people needed to assimilate into white society, giving up their traditional ways to become like Euro-Americans in their living arrangements, dress, pastimes, religious expression, and work.

The government tried to achieve assimilation in many ways. One was to divide certain reservations into individual parcels of land for male-headed families to own and farm. A federal policy since 1887, this process drastically reduced the size of the affected reservations and saw the transfer of land from Indian hands to those of whites. A second government policy required Indian children to attend boarding schools a great distance from their homes, where school staff tried to make them look, speak, and pray like white children.

These policies largely came to an end in 1934 with the passage of the Indian Reorganization Act (IRA), which replaced assimilation programs with initiatives that attempted to strengthen the tribes. Part of the "Indian New Deal," this legislation was spurred by a 1928 Brookings Institution report that found terrible poverty on reservations across the United States.

_____

An excerpt from 'Reservations, Resistance, and the Indian Reorganization Act, 1900-1940' by Catherine Denial

1. What is the precise topic of the passage?

a. Boarding schools for American Indians

b. American Indians

c. The forced assimilation of the American Indians

d. The American Indians lived on reservations

2. Which sentence from the excerpt best supports your answer to question 1?

a. Most lived on reservations—parcels of land that Indian people had retained in treaty negotiations.

b. The policy of the federal government was that American Indian people needed to assimilate into white society.

c. A second government policy required Indian children to attend boarding schools.

d. The federal census recorded just over 200,000 American Indian people living in the United States.

3. Circle the main idea.

a. American Indians were required to assimilate into Euro-American society.

b. The American Indians lost their land to Euro-Americans.

c. Most American Indians lived on reservations.

d. All American Indian children were required to attend boarding schools ran by Euro-Americans.

4. Identify the major supporting detail below.

a. There was terrible poverty on reservations across the United States.

b. The Indian Reorganization Act (IRA) replaced assimilation programs.

c. The assimilation policies largely came to an end in 1934.

d. American Indians needed to give up their traditional ways to become like Euro-Americans.

5. Which of the following is the best summary of the article?

a. American Indian children were required to attend boarding schools so they could assimilate into Euro-American society.

b. The federal government attempted to seize as much land as possible from the American Indians.

c. The federal government tried different ways of forcing American Indians to assimilate into Euro-American society until the Indian Reorganization Act was passed.

d. The Indian Reorganization Act of 1934 strengthened American Indian tribes.

Passage 2

During the late 1800s and early 1900s, the Temperance Movement fought to reduce consumption of alcohol. The movement began in the 1820s, rooted in Protestant churches, led by clergy and prominent laymen, and powered by women volunteers. More women were involved in temperance than any other cause in US history up to that point. Women's involvement seemed natural since the movement targeted men's alcohol abuse and how it harmed women and children. At first, the Temperance Movement sought to moderate drinking, then to promote resisting the temptation to drink. Later, the goal became outright prohibition of alcohol sales. This shift coincided with a large wave of immigrants from Southern, Central, and Eastern Europe, and some temperance advocates echoed the concerns of nativists as they objected to immigrants' "wet" cultures and drinking customs. In addition, temperance advocates regarded urban saloons as hosts to a range of immoral behaviors beyond drunkenness, such as gambling, adultery, prostitution, profanity, and corruption.

Women rose to leadership roles with the founding of the national Woman's Christian Temperance Union (WCTU) in 1874. Temperance became known as the "Woman's Crusade," and women staged peaceful demonstrations of prayer at businesses that served alcohol. These methods reflected the gentle moral guidance expected from women of the era. Later, the Temperance Movement changed its goals and tactics, and it became a powerful political force which sought to prohibit alcohol entirely.

———

An excerpt from 'Women and the Temperance Movement' by Melissa Strong

Write a summary of the passage.
(Remember, your summary should include your main idea and one or two major supporting details.)

Summary: _____

_____

_____

REFLECTION ON LEARNING

Answer the following reflection questions and feel free to discuss your responses with your teacher or a classmate.

- What reading idea or strategy did you learn from this section?

- What new concepts did you learn?

- What methods did you work on in this section?

- What aspect of this section is still not 100 percent clear for you?

- What do you want your teacher to know?

LESSON 5
DRAWING INFERENCES

By the end of this lesson, you will be able to make inferences about images and texts.

An **inference** is a conclusion you make based on the facts and evidence that you have. In other words, drawing inferences means "making an educated guess" since you use clues to figure out what you don't know.

Here are some ways you can draw inferences from images and texts.

USE BACKGROUND KNOWLEDGE.

Remember, your background or prior knowledge is your knowledge and experiences that help you understand texts and images. Study the text or image carefully and use your background knowledge to make a conclusion. Note that more than one correct answer is possible.

Let's study the following examples.

SCENARIO 1

You are about to go out when you realize that one of your shoes is missing. You find it behind the couch with teeth marks on it.

What do you know?

✓ Your dog likes chewing shoes and other items.
✓ Your dog knows it's wrong to chew your belongings.
✓ Your shoe has teeth marks.

What do you infer?

Your dog hid behind the couch to chew your shoes so he wouldn't get caught.

SCENARIO 2

You are waiting for the train when you notice a man, dressed in business attire, holding a briefcase. He keeps pacing and checking his watch.

What do you know?

✓ People wear business attire for work, meetings, formal functions and interviews.
✓ Briefcases often hold formal documents.
✓ People check watches often when they're anxious about something relating to time.
✓ People pace when they're thinking, anxious or upset.

What do you infer?

The man is worried about arriving late to either work, a meeting or an interview.

SCENARIO 3

You are a courier delivering a package to a house. On the porch, there are toys inside the flower pot. When a woman opens the door, she is holding a baby bottle.

What do you know?

_____

_____

What do you infer?

_____

_____

Do you understand inferences now? You use your observation skills and background knowledge to decide what is happening.

Now, let's try to figure out what's going on in the following pictures. Remember, more than one answer can be correct!

PICTURE 1

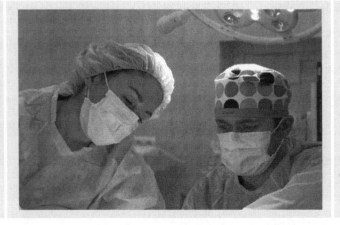

WHAT DO YOU KNOW?

- ✓ Doctors wear masks and protective gear when treating patients.
- ✓ Both doctors are looking down.
- ✓ Patients lie down during surgery.

WHAT DO YOU INFER?

This picture shows two surgeons performing surgery.

PICTURE 2

What do you know?

- ✓ People use laptops for work, school, entertainment and communication.
- ✓ Laptops malfunction sometimes.
- ✓ When people bow and grip their heads, they are sad, angry or frustrated.

What do you infer?

The picture is showing a woman who is frustrated while working because her laptop is malfunctioning.

PICTURE 3

What do you know?

✓ Maps are used to view the location of places.
✓ Tents are used for outdoor camping.

What do you infer?

_____

_____

_____

Look at the pictures below and make inferences about them.

PICTURE 4

What do you know?

_____

_____

What do you infer?

_____

_____

_____

PICTURE 5

What do you know?

_____

_____

What do you infer?

_____

_____

_____

You can make inferences about **texts** using your background knowledge and the text's details or **context clues**.

Read the passage below and answer the questions that follow.

PASSAGE 1

If a breath of air stirred, it made no sound here; for there was not a holly, not an evergreen to rustle, and the stripped hawthorn and hazel bushes were as still as the white, worn stones which causewayed the middle of the path.

———

An excerpt from *Jane Eyre* by Charlotte Bronte

Question: In which season is the story set?

Step 1: Search for context clues.
There was "not an evergreen to rustle," the bushes were "stripped," and the stones were "white and worn."

Step 2: Be a detective.
Ask yourself, "In which season do trees become bare and stones may look white?"

Step 3: Use your prior knowledge
I know that trees become bare and it snows during winter.

Step 4: Make an inference.
I can conclude that the passage is set in winter because it describes bare trees and white stones.

PASSAGE 2

The dressing process was one which taught them both something. Martha had "buttoned up" her little sisters and brothers but she had never seen a child who stood still and waited for another person to do things for her as if she had neither hands nor feet of her own.

"Why doesn't tha' put on tha' own shoes?" she said when Mary quietly held out her foot.

"My Ayah did it," answered Mary, staring. "It was the custom."

She said that very often—"It was the custom." The native servants were always saying it. If one told them to do a thing their ancestors had not done for a thousand years they gazed at one mildly and said, "It is not the custom" and one knew that was the end of the matter.

It had not been the custom that Mistress Mary should do anything but stand and allow herself to be dressed like a doll, but before she was ready for breakfast she began to suspect that her life at Misselthwaite Manor would end by teaching her a number of things quite new to her—things such as putting on her own shoes and stockings, and picking up things she let fall. If Martha had been a well-trained fine young lady's maid she would have been more subservient and respectful and would have known that it was her business to brush hair, and button boots, and pick things up and lay them away. She was, however, only an untrained Yorkshire rustic who had been brought up in a moorland cottage with a swarm of little brothers and sisters who had never dreamed of doing anything but waiting on themselves and on the younger ones who were either babies in arms or just learning to totter about and tumble over things.

———

An excerpt from *The Secret Garden* by Frances Hodgson Burnett

Question 1: What can you infer about Mary's life before she arrived at Misselthwaite Manor?

Step 1: Search for context clues.
At the manor, she does not dress herself or clean up after herself. She also refers to the "native servants" that she had before.

Step 2: Be a detective.
Ask yourself, "What kind of persons have servants that dress them?"

Step 3: Use your prior knowledge
Persons who are wealthy and overindulged.

Step 4: Make an inference.
Before living in the manor, Mary was overindulged and lived an upper-class life.

Now it's your turn. Read the passage on the next page and answer the question that follows.
(Hint: Use context clues such as the title and image to help you.)

PASSAGE 3

COTTON GIN AND THE EXPANSION OF SLAVERY

The invention of the cotton gin forever altered the economy, geography, and politics of the United States. The cotton gin made cotton tremendously profitable, which encouraged westward migration to new areas of the US South to grow more cotton. The number of enslaved people rose with the increase in cotton production, from 700,000 in 1790 to over three million by 1850. By mid-century, the southern states were responsible for seventy-five percent of the world's cotton, most of which was shipped to New England or England, where it was made into cloth. Whitney's cotton gin and its descendants helped the southern states become a major agricultural force in the world economy on the backs of a growing enslaved population.

After the Civil War, cotton production boomed, as many newly emancipated African Americans continued to work in cotton fields as sharecroppers—tenants who rented land from farmers in return for a share of the crops harvested from that land. In the sharecropping system, landowners often cheated tenants using financial deception reinforced by racial violence to keep sharecroppers working to pay off endless debt. By the 1950s, mechanized cotton pickers had largely replaced manual cotton picking, but modern versions of the cotton gin are still in use today.

What was the cotton gin?

Context clues:

_____

Prior knowledge:

_____

Inference:

_____

PRACTICE EXERCISES

Read the passage and answer the questions that follow.

PASSAGE 4

ANNE'S BRINGING-UP IS BEGUN

For reasons best known to herself, Marilla did not tell Anne that she was to stay at Green Gables until the next afternoon. During the forenoon she kept the child busy with various tasks and watched over her with a keen eye while she did them. By noon she had concluded that Anne was smart and obedient, willing to work and quick to learn; her most serious **shortcoming** seemed to be a tendency to fall into daydreams in the middle of a task and forget all about it until such time as she was sharply recalled to earth by a reprimand or a catastrophe.

When Anne had finished washing the dinner dishes she suddenly confronted Marilla with the air and expression of one desperately determined to learn the worst. Her thin little body trembled from head to foot; her face flushed and her eyes dilated until they were almost black; she clasped her hands tightly and said in an imploring voice:

"Oh, please, Miss Cuthbert, won't you tell me if you are going to send me away or not? I've tried to be patient all the morning, but I really feel that I cannot bear not knowing any longer. It's a dreadful feeling. Please tell me."

"You haven't scalded the dishcloth in clean hot water as I told you to do," said Marilla immovably. "Just go and do it before you ask any more questions, Anne."

Anne went and attended to the dishcloth. Then she returned to Marilla and fastened imploring eyes of the latter's face. "Well," said Marilla, unable to find any excuse for deferring her explanation longer, "I suppose I might as well tell you. Matthew and I have decided to keep you—that is, if you will try to be a good little girl and show yourself grateful. Why, child, whatever is the matter?"

"I'm crying," said Anne in a tone of bewilderment.

Excerpt from *Anne of Green Gables* by L.M. Montgomery

1. What is happening in the excerpt? Choose the best description.

    a. Marilla is deciding whether to keep Anne or not.

    b. Marilla is delaying telling Anne that she can stay at Green Gables.

    c. Anne is daydreaming.

    d. Anne is unsuccessfully completing her chores.

2. Why do you think Marilla does not tell Anne that she can stay at Green Gables?

    a. She wants to punish Anne for her mishaps.

    b. She was too busy to speak with Anne.

    c. She wants the news to be a surprise.

    d. She wants to be sure that she is making the best decision.

3. When Marilla tells Anne that she can stay, Anne begins crying. Which of the following is the best inference for her emotional reaction?

    a. Anne becomes overwhelmed with joy.

    b. Anne is terrified of Marilla.

    c. Anne is furious that she has to stay.

    d. Anne is depressed that she is to stay at Green Gables.

4. Which sentence below would be the best inference of what "Green Gables" is?

    a. Anne's orphanage

    b. Marilla's home

    c. Anne's home

    d. The porch

5. Read the line from the passage: "...her most serious **shortcoming** seemed to be a tendency to fall into daydreams in the middle of a task."
    What is the meaning of the word "shortcoming?"

    a. A person's strength

    b. Someone's prized possession

    c. A special talent

    d. A fault or weakness in someone

Study the picture below.

Make an inference about what is happening in the picture.

Context Clues

_____

_____

_____

Prior knowledge

_____

_____

_____

Inference

_____

_____

_____

REFLECTION ON LEARNING

Answer the following reflection questions and feel free to discuss your responses with your teacher or a classmate.

- What reading idea or strategy did you learn from this section?

- What new concepts did you learn?

- What methods did you work on in this section?

- What aspect of this section is still not 100 percent clear for you?

- What do you want your teacher to know?

LESSON 6

COMPREHENSION MONITORING

By the end of this lesson, you will be able to use strategies to monitor your comprehension of texts.

Comprehension monitoring means being able to check in with yourself and know if you're understanding a text or not. It includes the following skills:

- Knowing what you **do** understand
- Identifying what you **do not** understand
- Using strategies to **improve** your understanding

Sometimes you may realize that you're not fully understanding what you're reading. When this happens, you can use certain methods to improve your understanding. These are called **"fix-up strategies."**

Here are the steps you can take while monitoring your comprehension.

1. **STOP** after a few sentences or at the end of a paragraph or page.

   - Ask yourself, "Is this making sense to me?"
   - Check if you can state the main points of what you've read so far.
   - If you can, continue reading. If not, go onto Step 2.

2. **THINK** and ask yourself:

   - When did I lose track?
   - Do I not understand the meaning of a word?
   - Do I not know enough about the topic?
   - Did I become distracted?

3. **REACT** by using the best **fix-up strategy** to fix your problem.

   - Reread the part.
   - Use your background knowledge.
   - Research the meaning of the unknown word or try to figure out the meaning using context clues.
   - Find out more about the topic.
   - Look at images, headlines, transitions, etc. that may help you.
   - Create mental images in your mind.
   - Ask for help.

PRACTICE EXERCISE

Read the following passage. While reading, use the comprehension monitoring strategies to help you understand the passage.

The Unproductive Farm

When a soil expert visits an unproductive farm to determine its needs, he gives his chief attention to four possible factors in his problem: lack of drainage, of lime, of organic matter, and of available plant-food. His first concern regards drainage. If the water from rains is held in the surface by an impervious stratum beneath, it is idle to spend money in other amendments until the difficulty respecting drainage has been overcome. A water-logged soil is helpless. It cannot provide available plant-food, air, and warmth to plants. Under-drainage is urgently demanded when the level of dead water in the soil is near the surface. The area needing drainage is larger than most land-owners believe, and it increases as soils become older. On the other hand, the requirements of lime, organic matter, and available plant-food are so nearly universal, in the case of unproductive land in the eastern half of the United States, that they are here given prior consideration, and drainage is discussed in another place when methods of controlling soil moisture are described. The production of organic matter is so important to depleted soils, and is so dependent upon the absence of soil acidity, that the right use of lime on land claims our first interest.

Lime performs various offices in the soil, but farmers should be concerned chiefly about only one, and that is the destruction of acids and poisons that make the soil unfriendly to most forms of plant life, including the clovers, alfalfa, and other legumes. Lime was put into all soils by nature. Large areas were originally very rich in lime, while other areas of the eastern half of the United States never were well supplied. Within the last ten years it has been definitely determined that a large part of this vast territory has an actual lime deficiency, as measured by its inability to remain alkaline or "sweet." Many of the noted limestone valleys show marked soil acidity.

Excerpt from *Crops and Methods for Soil Improvement* by Alva Agee

LESSON 7
QUESTION-ANSWER RELATIONSHIPS

By the end of this lesson, you will be able to use the question-answer strategy to find and understand information.

Self-questioning is the process of asking yourself questions **before, during** and **after** reading a text. This skill is important as you can keep yourself in check and know if you're understanding and thinking critically about what you're reading.

Question- answer relationship (QAR) shows a relationship between the question, text and reader. It teaches you the **types** of questions to ask in order to understand the text better. It also helps you to answer certain kinds of questions efficiently.

Why use QAR?

- ✓ It improves reading comprehension.
- ✓ It shows you how to find the answers to questions.
- ✓ It encourages you to use critical thinking skills.

There are **three** types of QAR questions.

1. **"Right there"** or literal questions: The answers can be found directly in the text. Often, the words of the questions and those in the text are the same.
2. **"Think and search"** or inference questions: The answers may be found in different parts of the text. You may also need to use analysis and context clues to figure out the answers. The questions use different words than the ones in the text.
3. **"On my own"** or evaluative questions: The answers are not found in the text. Instead, you must use your knowledge and judgment to answer the questions.

EXAMPLE 1

In the mid-eighteenth century, present-day California was the northernmost Spanish colony on the North American continent. In 1769, on orders from Spain's King Charles III, Gaspar de Portolá and a group of Franciscans led by Junípero Serra traveled from Baja California to explore territory to the North. Their goal was to extend the missions (or religious settlements) from Baja California into the area that would become Alta California by establishing a string of new outposts a day's journey apart.

From 1769 to 1833, Spanish Franciscans established twenty-one missions in Alta California, stretching 600 miles from San Diego to San Francisco along a path eventually known as the "California Mission Trail." The goal of these settlements was twofold: to protect Spanish colonial interests in the new world and to "civilize," educate, and convert Native Americans into tax-paying Spanish colonial citizens. In this way, Spanish mission work in Alta California mirrored the goals and efforts of the Spanish mission project throughout its colonies in the New World. Initially, these missions were meant to be self-sufficient, but they did not achieve this goal and instead relied on financial assistance from Spain.

The impact of the missions on Native American populations was devastating. According to mission records, Franciscans at missions baptized more than 53,000 adult Native Americans and buried 37,000 during the period. Many Native Americans died from diseases such as measles and smallpox, introduced by Europeans, to which indigenous populations had no immunities.

An excerpt from 'Spanish Missions in California' by Franky Abbott

	QUESTION	ANSWER
LITERAL	What is the "California Mission Trail?"	It is a path of missions stretching 600 miles from San Diego to San Francisco.
	How many missions were established in Alta California?	Twenty-one missions were established in Alta California.
INFERENTIAL	Did the Spanish think of the Native Americans as developed people? Explain.	No, they did not because the passage states that the missions' purpose was to "civilize and educate" the Native Americans.
	Did the Spanish only focus their efforts in California?	No, the passage states that they had similar goals throughout colonies in the New World.
EVALUATIVE	Why do you think Spain assisted the mission in "civilizing" the Native Americans?	I think they did this in hopes that the Native Americans would be able to pay taxes to Spain.
	Why did they establish many missions in Alta California?	They established many missions so more Native Americans would become colonial citizens.

EXAMPLE 2

	QUESTION	ANSWER
LITERAL	What are the men doing in the picture?	They are collecting hay.
INFERENTIAL	What is the purpose of the animals?	The animals are being used to transport the hay.
EVALUATIVE	Do you think the animals are necessary?	Yes, I think the animals are necessary as the men may not have the energy and strength to transport that amount of hay manually. Additionally, they may not have access to machinery to do the job.

Can you think of other questions for the passage and picture?

PRACTICE EXERCISES

Read the passage below and answer the questions that follow.

He had taken me aside one day and promised me a silver fourpenny on the first of every month if I would only keep my "weather eye open for a seafaring man with one leg," and let him know the moment he appeared. Often enough when the first of the month came round, and I applied to him for my wage, he would only blow through his nose at me, and stare me down; but before the week was out he was sure to think better of it, bring me my fourpenny piece, and repeat his orders to look out for "the seafaring man with one leg."

How that personage haunted my dreams, I need scarcely tell you. On stormy nights, when the wind shook the four corners of the house, and the surf roared along the cove and up the cliffs, I would see him in a thousand forms, and with a thousand diabolical expressions. Now the leg would be cut off at the knee, now at the hip; now he was a monstrous kind of a creature who had never had but one leg, and that in the middle of his body. To see him leap and run and pursue me over hedge and ditch, was the worst of nightmares. And altogether I paid pretty dear for my monthly fourpenny piece, in the shape of these abominable fancies.

But though I was so terrified by the idea of the seafaring man with one leg, I was far less afraid of the captain himself than anybody else who knew him. There were nights when he took a deal more rum and water than his head would carry; and then he would sometimes sit and sing his wicked, old, wild sea-songs, minding nobody; but sometimes he would call for glasses round and force all the trembling company to listen to his stories or bear a chorus to his singing. Often I have heard the house shaking with "Yo-ho-ho, and a bottle of rum," all the neighbors joining in for dear life, with the fear of death upon them, and each singing louder than the other to avoid remark. For in these fits he was the most overriding companion ever known; he would slap his hand on the table for silence all round; he would fly up in a passion of anger at a question, or sometimes because none was put, and so he judged the company was not following his story. Nor would he allow anyone to leave the inn till he had drunk himself sleepy and reeled off to bed.

_____

An excerpt from *Treasure Island* by Robert Louis Stevenson

LITERAL

1. What was the narrator required to do to gain a fourpenny piece each month?

   a. He was to notify the captain each time the seafaring man appeared.

   b. He was to capture the seafaring man.

   c. He was to stand lookout for the seafaring man.

   d. He was to guard the ship against the seafaring man.

INFERENTIAL

2. Why were people afraid of the captain?

   a. He asked people to sing with him.

   b. He would get drunk and fly into a fit of rage with his crew.

   c. He threatened his crew with the seafaring man.

   d. He would get drunk and threaten to cut off peoples' legs if they did not entertain him.

EVALUATIVE

3. Which statement best describes the captain's personality?

a. He is ill-tempered but keeps his word.

b. He is a fair and generous person.

c. He is a humorous and sociable man.

d. He is generally kind but ill-tempered when drunk.

Study the picture below and answer the questions that follow.

Literal

1. What issue is the picture mainly highlighting?

a. The disregard for the homeless

b. Toxic relationships

c. Child abuse

d. Global warming

Inferential

2. What is most likely the reason that the person in the picture is barefooted?

a. It is not permitted for persons to wear shoes.

b. Someone stole her shoes.

c. Her feet hurt, so she chose not to wear shoes.

d. She cannot afford a pair of shoes.

Evaluative

3. How do you think the person sitting on the ground must feel?

a. Cheerful

b. Energetic

c. Hopeless

d. Excited

REFLECTION ON LEARNING

Answer the following reflection questions and feel free to discuss your responses with your teacher or a classmate.

- What reading idea or strategy did you learn from this section?

- What new concepts did you learn?

- What methods did you work on in this section?

- What aspect of this section is still not 100 percent clear for you?

- What do you want your teacher to know?

LESSON 8
THE IMPORTANCE OF TEXT STRUCTURE

By the end of this lesson, you will be able to identify and analyze the following text structures:

- Description
- Sequence or Chronology
- Cause and effect
- Compare and contrast
- Problem-solution

Text structure refers to the way information in a text is organized by the writer. Writers may use one type of structure or combine structures for fiction and nonfiction texts. Let's examine the common types of structures.

1. **Description**

The writer uses this structure to give detailed descriptions of ideas, sceneries, events, persons and things. Therefore, the text has many adjectives and details.

Signal words: such as, for example, specifically, in particular, additionally, characteristics

Example:

Margaret, the eldest of the four, was sixteen, and very pretty, being plump and fair, with large eyes, plenty of soft brown hair, a sweet mouth, and white hands, of which she was rather vain. Fifteen-year-old Jo was very tall, thin, and brown, and reminded one of a colt, for she never seemed to know what to do with her long limbs, which were very much in her way. She had a decided mouth, a comical nose, and sharp, gray eyes, which appeared to see everything, and were by turns fierce, funny, or thoughtful. Her long, thick hair was her one beauty, but it was usually bundled into a net, to be out of her way. Round shoulders had Jo, big hands and feet, a flyaway look to her clothes, and the uncomfortable appearance of a girl who was rapidly shooting up into a woman and didn't like it. Elizabeth, or Beth, as everyone called her, was a rosy, smooth-haired, bright-eyed girl of thirteen, with a shy manner, a timid voice, and a peaceful expression which was seldom disturbed. Her father called her 'Little Miss Tranquility', and the name suited her excellently, for she seemed to live in a happy world of her own, only venturing out to meet the few whom she trusted and loved. Amy, though the youngest, was a most important person, in her own opinion at least. A regular snow maiden, with blue eyes, and yellow hair curling on her shoulders, pale and slender, and always carrying herself like a young lady mindful of her manners. What the characters of the four sisters were we will leave to be found out.

An excerpt from *Little Women* by Louisa May Alcott

This text is descriptive as it gives details of the sister's appearances. The organizer on the next page can be used to organize the descriptive details in a text.

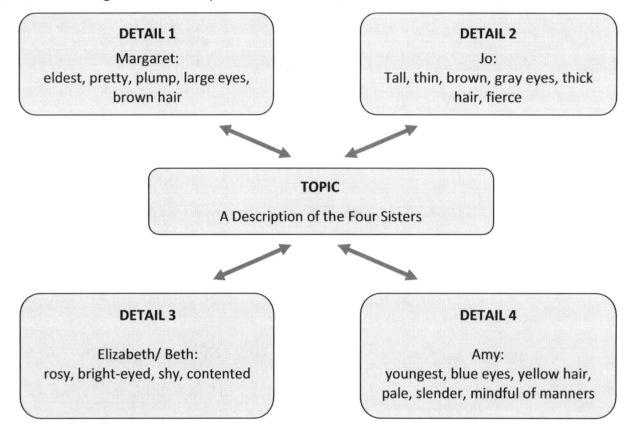

DETAIL 1
Margaret:
eldest, pretty, plump, large eyes, brown hair

DETAIL 2
Jo:
Tall, thin, brown, gray eyes, thick hair, fierce

TOPIC
A Description of the Four Sisters

DETAIL 3
Elizabeth/ Beth:
rosy, bright-eyed, shy, contented

DETAIL 4
Amy:
youngest, blue eyes, yellow hair, pale, slender, mindful of manners

2. **Sequence or Chronology**

Using this structure, writers list the steps in a process or provide information on events in the order that they occurred.

Signal words: First, second, next, then, before, after, finally, while, dates

Example:

In making Green tea, the object seems to be to expel the watery juices of the leaf and to cure or dry it with the least delay. Hence, the leaves are not exposed to the sun, but are first dried in the air for a short time. They are next exposed to artificial heat, which renders them flaccid and pliable, and prepares them for the third operation of rolling, which twists the yielding leaf as seen in manufactured tea, rolls it up into balls, and squeezes out a considerable portion of its watery juices. It is a singular fact that in the Chinese methods, they endeavor to get rid of the exuding juices, while in the Indian treatment, according to Mr. Crole, the manufacturing expert, effort is made to preserve the sappy juice, and it is continually taken up again by the balls of leaves. The balls are now broken apart, and the scattered leaves are submitted to the final drying process by fire, which finishes Green tea. In this case, it is plainly the heating treatment which develops the faint flavor and odor of Green tea, for no fermentation is allowed to begin, unless indeed brief and unobserved action takes place within the compressed balls.

_____
An excerpt from *Tea Leaves* by Francis H. Leggett & Co.

In this excerpt, the writer effectively uses a sequence structure to give the reader the steps in making green tea.

Write the main details of each step in the sequence graphic organizer below.

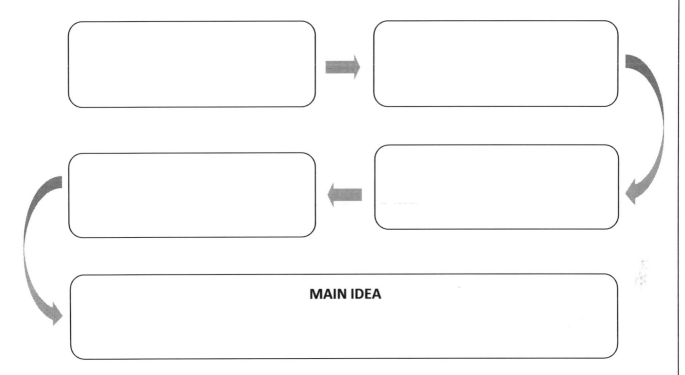

3. **Cause and Effect**

Using cause and effect structures, writers help readers understand by giving the reasons for an occurrence (causes) and the events that follow (effects).

Signal Words: due to, because of, led to, since, as a result, consequently, therefore, reasons

There can be more than one cause and one effect.

Example:

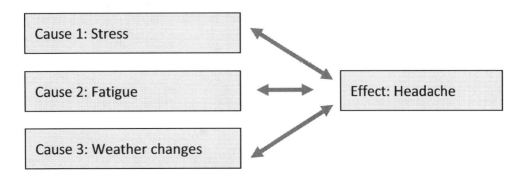

There can also be one cause or source with different outcomes.

Example:

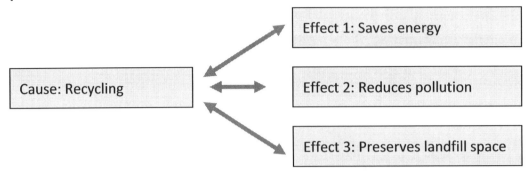

Cause: Recycling

Effect 1: Saves energy

Effect 2: Reduces pollution

Effect 3: Preserves landfill space

Now let's read the cause-and-effect passage below.

Historical evidence proves that there were interactions between Europe and the Americas before Christopher Columbus's voyage in 1492. But Columbus's contact precipitated a large, impactful, and lastingly significant transfer of animals, crops, people groups, cultural ideas, and microorganisms between the two worlds. In 1493, for example, on his second voyage, Columbus brought horses, dogs, pigs, cattle, chickens, sheep, and goats to the "new" world. Later in the 1530s, the Spanish conquistador and explorer Francisco Pizarro saw the potato in the Andes of South America and brought this crop to Europe. Bacteria and viruses, as well technological and cultural ideas, moved between the hemispheres, and Europeans forcibly transported enslaved people from Africa to the Americas to provide free labor. These transfers had a monumental impact on the development of our modern world. Alfred Crosby, who wrote an important 1972 book called The Columbian Exchange: Biological and Cultural Consequences of 1492, asserts that the commingling of plants, animals, and bacteria resulting from the Columbian Exchange is one of the most important ecological events in human history.

_____

An excerpt from The Colombian Exchange by Jamie Lathan

Complete the organizer below by inserting the cause and effects described in the passage.

MAIN IDEA

CAUSE	EFFECT

4. **Compare and Contrast**

Writers can use compare and contrast structures to show how two or more events, people, ideas, etc. are different and similar.

Signal words: unlike, similar to, alike, different, both, however, comparable, both, although

Example:

Abraham Lincoln and Frederick Douglass were both great men who rose from poverty to become advocates for freedom and equality. Although their backgrounds are seemingly different and their meetings brief, their work to end slavery is undeniable. Lincoln, born in 1809 to poor farmers in Kentucky, moved to Illinois, earned a law degree and was elected to state and national-level office. Douglass was born into slavery in Maryland. After Douglass's escape, he became an ardent abolitionist, publishing his autobiography and a weekly abolitionist newspaper entitled The North Star. These men met three separate times during Lincoln's presidency to discuss issues such as the Emancipation Proclamation and the Thirteenth Amendment. When Douglass was turned away from the White House on the day of Lincoln's Second Inauguration, Lincoln called him back, saying, "There is no man in the country whose opinion I value more than yours."

An excerpt from 'Frederick Douglass and Abraham Lincoln' by Albert Robertson and Adena Barnette.

The excerpt explains the similarities and differences between Frederick Douglass and Abraham Lincoln.

MAIN IDEA	
SIMILARITIES	**DIFFERENCES**

Write the main details in the table below.

5. **Problem-Solution**

In this type of text structure, the writer identifies a problem and explains solutions for the problem. The text can be complex as the writer may use descriptions to describe the problem and use steps, such as in a sequence structure, when giving the solution. The key is to focus on the **main idea** the writer is telling us.

Signal words: therefore, because of, reasons why, leads to consequently, a solution, a problem

Example:

Drainage

Productive soils are in a condition to admit air freely. The presence of air in the soil is as necessary to the changes producing availability of plant-food as it is to the changes essential to life in the human body. A water-logged soil is a worthless one in respect to the production of most valuable plants. The well-being of soil and plants requires that the level of dead water be a considerable distance below the surface.

When a soil has recently grown trees, the rotting stump roots leave cavities in the subsoil that permit the removal of some surplus water, and the rotted wood and leaves that give distinctive character to new land are absorbents of such water. As land becomes older, losing natural means of drainage and the excellent physical condition due to vegetable matter in it, the need of drainage grows greater. The tramping of horses in the bottoms of furrows made by breaking-plows often makes matters worse. The prompt removal of excessive moisture by drains, and preferably by underdrains, is essential to profitable farming in the case of most wet lands. The only exception is the land on which may be grown the grasses that thrive fairly well under moist conditions.

An excerpt from *Crops and Methods for Soil Improvement* by Alva Agee, M.S.

In this passage, the writer explains the problems caused by water-logged soil and explains how drainage can solve this problem.

Use the information in the passage to complete the organizer below.

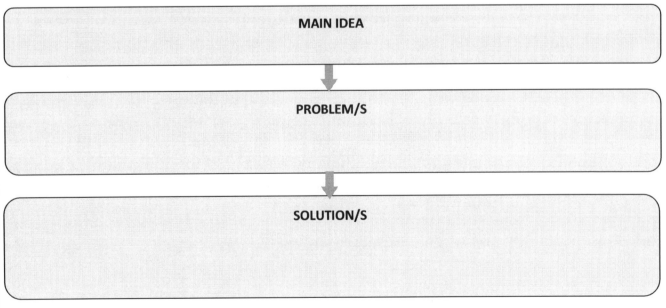

MAIN IDEA

PROBLEM/S

SOLUTION/S

PRACTICE EXERCISE

Read the following passage and answer the questions that follow.

Revolutionary War Turning Points: Saratoga and Valley Forge

After the start of the American Revolutionary War, the British attempted a two-pronged military strategy: divide New England from the rest of the states by seizing the Hudson River, and occupy the south by driving the rebels out the Carolinas and Virginia.

Intent on the first, British General John Burgoyne led a force of eight thousand troops southward through the Hudson valley towards the town of Saratoga, New York during the summer and fall of 1777. On September 19 and again on October 7, American forces led by General Horatio Gates clashed with the British Army. By October 8, the British forces totaled less than five thousand. The American Continentals pursued, and on October 17, twenty thousand surrounded the British, leaving Burgoyne with no choice other than to formally surrender. This decisive victory at Saratoga helped persuade the French to enter the war in February 1778, providing the money, supplies, and troops needed to turn the tide to American victory.

Farther south, British General William Howe sought to capture the American capital of Philadelphia. The British invaded from the south, via Chesapeake Bay, and defeated George Washington's troops in the Battle of Brandywine on September 11, 1777. American troops under Washington then lost control of Philadelphia. Washington and his ten thousand soldiers finally retreated twenty-four miles to the west, where they set up headquarters at the village of Valley Forge. There Washington's troops survived a difficult winter of disease, freezing temperatures, and a continual lack of supplies.

———

An excerpt from 'Revolutionary War Turning Points: Saratoga and Valley Forge' by Adena Barnette

1. British General John Burgoyne surrendered because…

    a. American forces outnumbered his army.
    b. The French had entered the war.
    c. He was trying to fool the Americans by pretending to surrender.
    d. The Americans promised resources if he did.

2. Which is the main reason that the French entered the war?

    a. They were promised money, supplies and troops.
    b. They saw that it was possible for American forces to win.
    c. The British had wronged them during the American Revolutionary War.
    d. They wanted to rule England.

3. Circle the statement that best states the precise topic of the passage.

   a. The British forces against the American forces during the Revolutionary War
   b. The American Revolutionary War
   c. General John Burgoyne and General Horatio Gates
   d. The Defeat of George Washington's troops during the Revolutionary War

4. Identify the main idea of the passage.

   a. The American support outweighed the support for the British.
   b. The British tried two strategies during the Revolutionary War.
   c. The British and the Americans fought during the Revolutionary War.
   d. The Americans proved to be resilient during the Revolutionary War.

5. What kind of text structure does the writer **mainly** use in the passage?

   a. Description
   b. Sequence/ chronology
   c. Cause and effect
   d. Compare and contrast

6. What is the meaning of the phrase "two-pronged military strategy?"

   a. An attack that can be only ordered by two generals
   b. A strategy that involves two spies
   c. A military tactic that requires two kinds of resources
   d. A tactic that has two approaches to achieve victory

REFLECTION ON LEARNING

Answer the following reflection questions and feel free to discuss your responses with your teacher or a classmate.

- What reading idea or strategy did you learn from this section?

- What new concepts did you learn?

- What methods did you work on in this section?

- What aspect of this section is still not 100 percent clear for you?

- What do you want your teacher to know?

LESSON 9
FIGURING OUT FIGURATIVE LANGUAGE

By the end of this lesson, you will be able to identify and understand the use of similes, metaphors, personification and theme in texts.

Writers make stories, poems, songs, plays and even advertisements more relatable and understandable by using figurative language. Figurative language goes beyond literal or surface meanings. There are a wide variety of techniques writers use. Let's look at a few below.

Similes

A simile is the comparison between two different things that seem alike because of how the writer describes them. This comparison is made with the use of "like" or "as." You may know some of the common similes below.

Examples:

The athlete is **as quick as lightning**.

I was surprised that the package was **light like air**.

Martha was **as proud as a peacock** when she won the prize.

Kimberly was **like a bat** without her glasses.

COMPARISON (1)	SIMILE SIGN	COMPARISON (2)	ASPECT OF COMPARISON
The athlete	As	Lightning	Quickness
The package	Like	Air	Lightness (weight)
Martha	As	Peacock	Pride
Kimberly	Like	Bat	Poor eyesight

EXERCISE 1

Read the sentences below and complete the table for each.

1. Before the exam, Amanda looked **as anxious as her pet hamster**.
2. Dennis stuck to his brother **like a tick**.
3. Kerwin moves **like a snail** in the morning!
4. The man was **as brave as a lion** when he saved the children.
5. Angelo's face became **red like a beetroot** when he spotted Anne.

COMPARISON (1)	SIMILE SIGN	COMPARISON (2)	ASPECT OF COMPARISON
1.			
2.			
3.			
4.			
5.			

You can even find similes in popular songs.

"When times get rough
And friends just can't be found
Like a bridge over troubled water
I will lay me down"

An excerpt from "Bridge over Troubled Water"
by Simon and Garfunkel

In this part of the song, the singer compares himself to a bridge that his loved one can use to overcome difficult times.

Metaphors

Like similes, metaphors make comparisons between things that are not alike. However, it does not use "like" or "as" in the comparison. As it does not have signal words, metaphors are called **implied comparisons**. They may be a little tricky to spot!

Simile vs. Metaphor

Simile: The children's laughter was **like music to the soul**.
Metaphor: The children's laughter **was music to the soul**.

As you can see, the children's laughter is compared to music in both sentences. However, the connecting word "like" is used in the simile. Let's study more metaphors.

Examples:
Nella's home became a prison.
The ideas were water flowing through her mind.
Georgina endured a rollercoaster of emotions.
Marlene's visit was the icing on the cake for me.

COMPARISON (1)	COMPARISON (2)	ASPECT OF COMPARISON
Nella's home	Prison	Confinement, punishment
The ideas	Water	Flowing movement
Rollercoaster	Emotions	Ups and downs
Marlene's visit	Icing on cake	A good situation

Exercise 2

Read the sentences below and complete the table for each.

1. Paul is a night owl, so he will study tonight.
2. I gazed at the balls of cotton floating in the sky.
3. The volcano inside Christopher erupted as he shouted for justice.
4. Katherine is a couch potato during the weekend.
5. Books are the key to your imagination.

COMPARISON (1)	COMPARISON (2)	ASPECT OF COMPARISON

Read the quote below.

"All the world's a stage, and all the men and women merely players. They have their exits and their entrances."

_____

An excerpt from "As You Like It" by Shakespeare

Questions to consider:

1. What are the two things being compared?
2. What do you think the writer means by the metaphor?

Personification

Personification is the technique of giving human characteristics to something that isn't human, such as a feeling, an object or an idea. It makes things more understandable and relatable since we perceive the world as humans.

Examples:

1. *The abandoned house seemed depressed.*

In the example, an abandoned house is being described as having feelings, although we know that houses cannot feel. By adding this emotion, however, we can imagine how dilapidated the house looks.

2. *I was surprised when the opportunity came knocking on my door.*

While an opportunity cannot knock on anyone's door, it is used here to help the reader understand how opportunity can appear in front of you at any given moment.

3. *Tokyo is often described as the city that never sleeps.*
What human attribute is given to the city? Explain why this is done.

Exercise 3

1. Which of these quotes is an example of personification?

   a. When I looked up, the stars winked at me.
   b. Sometimes, love is a battlefield.
   c. Their friendship was as deep as the ocean.
   d. The memories were like water in cupped hands.

2. Underline the use of personification in the poem below.

> *I wandered lonely as a cloud*
> *That floats on high o'er vales and hills,*
> *When all at once I saw a crowd,*
> *A host, of golden daffodils;*
> *Beside the lake, beneath the trees,*
> *Fluttering and dancing in the breeze.*
> _____
> An excerpt from "I Wandered Lonely as a Cloud" by William Wordsworth

3. Read the excerpt below.

> But, on one side of the portal, and rooted almost at the threshold, was a wild rose-bush, covered, in this month of June, with its delicate gems, which might be imagined to offer their fragrance and fragile beauty to the prisoner as he went in, and to the condemned criminal as he came forth to his doom, in token that the deep heart of Nature could pity and be kind to him.
> _____
> An excerpt from "The Scarlet Letter" by Nathaniel Hawthorne

Explain what is being personified in the excerpt.

_____

_____

Identifying the Theme

The theme is the underlying message that the writer would like to deliver to the reader. It is different from the topic as the topic is generally **what** the story is about, whereas the theme is what the writer is **telling** us. There may be many themes in a writing piece.

Example:

Let's look at the poem below.

If I Can Stop One Heart from Breaking
By Emily Dickinson

If I can stop one heart from breaking,
I shall not live in vain;
If I can ease one life the aching,
Or cool one pain,
Or help one fainting robin
Unto his nest again,
I shall not live in vain.

Ask yourself, "What does the poet want to tell me in the poem?" Look for evidence.

In the poem, she states that if she helps others, she will not live in vain. Therefore, we can say that the message is that "selflessness can give life purpose."

EXERCISE 4

Read the poem below and answer the following questions.

Fall Leaves Fall
By Emily Bronte

Fall, leaves, fall; die, flowers, away;
Lengthen night and shorten day;
Every leaf speaks bliss to me
Fluttering from the autumn tree.

I shall smile when wreaths of snow
Blossom where the rose should grow;
I shall sing when night's decay
Ushers in a drearier day.

1. Which of the following best describes the theme of the poem?

    a. Nature can heal us.
    b. Winter is a dreary season.
    c. Winter can be a welcoming season.
    d. Flowers and leaves are useless.

2. What evidence best shows the theme that you chose in question 1?

    a. Leaves and flowers die.
    b. The leaves speak blissfully to the poet.
    c. The poet smiles and sings when winter comes.
    d. The days become shorter and the nights longer.

3. Identify the example of personification used in the poem.

    a. I shall smile when wreaths of snow blossom…
    b. I shall sing when night's decay…
    c. Lengthen night and shorten day…
    d. Every leaf speaks bliss to me…

PRACTICE EXERCISES

Poem

Read the poem below and answer the questions that follow.

Shadow March

By Robert Louis Stevenson

All round the house is the jet-black night;
It stares through the window-pane;
It crawls in the corners, hiding from the light,
And it moves with the moving flame.

Now my little heart goes a-beating like a drum,
With the breath of Bogie in my hair,
And all round the candle the crooked shadows come,
And go marching along up the stair.

The shadow of the balusters, the shadow of the lamp,
The shadow of the child that goes to bed—
All the wicked shadows coming, tramp, tramp, tramp,
With the black night overhead.

1. What is the poem describing?

    a. The fear of shadows during the night
    b. Shadows coming alive at night
    c. Ghosts and other creatures of the darkness
    d. A haunted house

2. "All round the house is the jet-black night;/ It stares through the window-pane"
   Which figurative device is used in the line above?

   a. Simile

   c. Personification

   b. Metaphor

   d. Theme

3. Identify an example of a simile used in the poem.

   a. It crawls in the corners, hiding from the light

   c. And all round the candle the crooked shadows come

   d. All the wicked shadows coming, tramp, tramp, tramp

   b. Now my little heart goes a-beating like a drum

PASSAGE

Read the passage below and answer the questions that follow.

No sooner did I see that his attention was riveted on them, and that I might gaze without being observed, than my eyes were drawn involuntarily to his face; I could not keep their lids under control: they would rise, and the iris would fix on him. I looked, and had an acute pleasure in looking,—a precious yet poignant pleasure; pure gold, with a steely point of agony: a pleasure like what the thirst-perishing man might feel who knows the well to which he has crept is poisoned, yet stoops and drinks divine draughts nevertheless.

Most true is it that "beauty is in the eye of the gazer." My master's colourless, olive face, square, massive brow, broad and jetty eyebrows, deep eyes, strong features, firm, grim mouth,—all energy, decision, will,—were not beautiful, according to rule; but they were more than beautiful to me; they were full of an interest, an influence that quite mastered me,—that took my feelings from my own power and fettered them in his. I had not intended to love him; the reader knows I had wrought hard to extirpate from my soul the germs of love there detected; and now, at the first renewed view of him, they spontaneously arrived, green and strong! He made me love him without looking at me.

I compared him with his guests. What was the gallant grace of the Lynns, the languid elegance of Lord Ingram,—even the military distinction of Colonel Dent, contrasted with his look of native pith and genuine power? I had no sympathy in their appearance, their expression: yet I could imagine that most observers would call them attractive, handsome, imposing; while they would pronounce Mr. Rochester at once harsh-featured and melancholy-looking. I saw them smile, laugh—it was nothing; the light of the candles had as much soul in it as their smile; the tinkle of the bell as much significance as their laugh. I saw Mr. Rochester smile:—his stern features softened; his eye grew both brilliant and gentle, its ray both searching and sweet.

_____

An excerpt from *Jane Eyre* by Charlotte Bronte

1. What is the theme developed in the passage?

   a. Beauty is in the eye of the gazer

   b. Beauty

   c. Unrequited love

   d. Love is brilliant

2. Which line best shows the theme of the passage?

   a. I saw Mr. Rochester smile... its ray both searching and sweet.

   b. Most true is it that "beauty is in the eye of the gazer."

   c. He made me love him without looking at me.

   d. I had not intended to love him

3. Which of the following is an example of a metaphor used in the passage?

   a. "...my eyes were drawn involuntarily to his face..."

   b. "...they spontaneously arrived, green and strong!"

   c. "...the light of the candles had as much soul in it as their smile..."

   d. "...I had wrought hard to extirpate from my soul the germs of love there detected..."

4. "...the tinkle of the bell as much significance as their laugh."
   What figurative device is used in the line above?

   a. Metaphor

   b. Simile

   c. Personification

   d. Theme

5. "At the first renewed view of him, they spontaneously arrived, green and strong!"
   Why does the narrator describe her love as "green and strong?"

   a. Because she is comparing love to strong poison

   b. Because she feels strongly about Mr. Rochester and she's jealous of him talking to others

   c. Because her favorite color is green

   d. Because she is comparing her newfound love to a fruit that is young and unripe

REFLECTION ON LEARNING

Answer the following reflection questions and feel free to discuss your responses with your teacher or a classmate.

- What reading idea or strategy did you learn from this section?

- What new concepts did you learn?

- What methods did you work on in this section?

- What aspect of this section is still not 100 percent clear for you?

- What do you want your teacher to know?

LESSON 10
EXAMINING POINT OF VIEW

By the end of this lesson, you will be able to determine the author's point of view through an examination of language use.

Point of view (POV) is the angle from which events are being told in a story. The **narrator** is the person telling the story in a book, while the **speaker** is the person relaying it in a poem. Neither the narrator nor the speaker refers to the actual writer.

When writing, an author would choose the best point of view to help the reader understand what is going on. Let's examine the main types of points of view.

1. **First-Person POV**

In this POV, the narrator relates the events directly from a "firsthand" experience. This POV can be identified by the use of the **first-person pronouns**: I, me, my, myself, mine, we, our, us and ourselves.

Example

> **I Heard You Solemn-Sweet Pipes of the Organ**
> By Walt Whitman
>
> I heard you solemn-sweet pipes of the organ as last Sunday morn I
> pass'd the church,
> Winds of autumn, as I walk'd the woods at dusk I heard your long-
> stretch'd sighs up above so mournful,
> I heard the perfect Italian tenor singing at the opera, I heard the
> soprano in the midst of the quartet singing;
> Heart of my love! you too I heard murmuring low through one of the
> wrists around my head,
> Heard the pulse of you when all was still ringing little bells last
> night under my ear

In the poem, the speaker is walking past a church and hears the organ. He speaks directly about his experiences, feelings and memories. This use of the first-person POV makes the reader feel connected with the speaker.

2. **Second-Person POV**

In this type of narration, the reader is a participant in the text. Therefore, the **second-person pronoun**, "**you**," is used. This POV is often used in instructional and informational texts.

Example

America's New Table Seasoning

Whether or not you salt your food, try adding the tang and aroma of fresh lemon juice. You know what lemons do for fish and seafood, tomato juice and tea. Now see what appetizing zest and sparkle they add to the many foods illustrated on this page.

A squeeze of lemon added right at the table brings out the full, natural flavors of the food itself. Lemon's tantalizing tang and wonderful "lemony" aroma stimulate the taste buds, make every bite taste better.

Serve a dish of lemon wedges right on the table every meal. Season all foods with fresh lemon juice—a marvelous aid to appetite.

Whether or *not* you salt your food, try adding the tang and aroma of fresh lemon juice. You know what lemons do for fish and seafood, tomato juice and tea. Now see what appetizing zest and sparkle they add to the many foods illustrated on this page.

———

An excerpt from "Salt...or No Salt" by Anonymous

In this text, the writer addresses the reader directly as he is giving instructions for the reader to follow.

A Question to Consider:

What are two actions that the writer is instructing the reader to do?

3. **Third-Person POV**

The third-person point of view occurs when the narrator is relaying the events as an **outsider.** This type of narration uses the **third-person pronouns**: he, she, him, her, they and them.

The two main types of third-person POV depend on how much the narrator accesses the character/s thoughts and feelings:

- **Limited Third-Person POV**

The narrator's perspective is *limited* to only one character's thoughts and feelings. The other characters are only perceived through that character.

Example

It was the White Rabbit, trotting slowly back again, and looking anxiously about as it went, as if it had lost something; and she heard it muttering to itself 'The Duchess! The Duchess! Oh my dear paws! Oh my fur and whiskers! She'll get me executed, as sure as ferrets are ferrets! Where can I have dropped them, I wonder?' Alice guessed in a moment that it was looking for the fan and the pair of white kid gloves, and she very good-naturedly began hunting about for them, but they were nowhere to be seen--everything seemed to have changed since her swim in the pool, and the great hall, with the glass table and the little door, had vanished completely.

Very soon the Rabbit noticed Alice, as she went hunting about, and called out to her in an angry tone, 'Why, Mary Ann, what are you doing out here? Run home this moment, and fetch me a pair of gloves and a fan! Quick, now!' And Alice was so much frightened that she ran off at once in the direction it pointed to, without trying to explain the mistake it had made.

"He took me for his housemaid," she said to herself as she ran. "How surprised he'll be when he finds out who I am! But I'd better take him his fan and gloves—that is, if I can find them." As she said this, she came upon a neat little house, on the door of which was a bright brass plate with the name "W. RABBIT," engraved upon it. She went in without knocking, and hurried upstairs, in great fear lest she should meet the real Mary Ann, and be turned out of the house before she had found the fan and gloves.

"How queer it seems," Alice said to herself, "to be going messages for a rabbit! I suppose Dinah'll be sending me on messages next!" And she began fancying the sort of thing that would happen: "'Miss Alice! Come here directly, and get ready for your walk!' 'Coming in a minute, nurse! But I've got to see that the mouse doesn't get out.' Only I don't think," Alice went on, "that they'd let Dinah stop in the house if it began ordering people about like that!"

An excerpt from *Alice's Adventures in Wonderland* by Lewis Carroll

In the example, the narrator only follows Alice's thoughts and feelings. The reader does not directly learn about the White Rabbit's thoughts or feelings or discovers what it does when Alice leaves him.

<u>**Questions to Consider:**</u>

1. How would you describe Alice's personality? Give a reason for your answer.
2. Why was Alice afraid to correct the White Rabbit?

- **Omniscient Third-Person POV**

"Omniscient" means "all-knowing," so, in the omniscient third-person point of view, the narrator knows what every character is thinking and feeling.

Example

The room in which the boys were fed, was a large stone hall, with a copper at one end: out of which the master, dressed in an apron for the purpose, and assisted by one or two women, ladled the gruel at mealtimes. Of this festive composition each boy had one porringer, and no more—except on occasions of great public rejoicing, when he had two ounces and a quarter of bread besides.

The bowls never wanted washing. The boys polished them with their spoons till they shone again; and when they had performed this operation (which never took very long, the spoons being nearly as large as the bowls), they would sit staring at the copper, with such eager eyes, as if they could have devoured the very bricks of which it was composed; employing themselves, meanwhile, in sucking their fingers most assiduously, with the view of catching up any stray splashes of gruel that might have been cast thereon. Boys have generally excellent appetites. Oliver Twist and his companions suffered the tortures of slow starvation for three months: at last they got so voracious and wild with hunger, that one boy, who was tall for his age, and hadn't been used to that sort of thing (for his father had kept a small cook-shop), hinted darkly to his companions, that unless he had another basin of gruel per diem, he was afraid he might some night happen to eat the boy who slept next him, who happened to be a weakly youth of tender age. He had a wild, hungry eye; and they implicitly believed him. A council was held; lots were cast who should walk up to the master after supper that evening, and ask for more; and it fell to Oliver Twist.

The evening arrived; the boys took their places. The master, in his cook's uniform, stationed himself at the copper; his pauper assistants ranged themselves behind him; the gruel was served out; and a long grace was said over the short commons. The gruel disappeared; the boys whispered each other, and winked at Oliver; while his next neighbors nudged him. Child as he was, he was desperate with hunger, and reckless with misery. He rose from the table; and advancing to the master, basin and spoon in hand, said: somewhat alarmed at his own temerity:

'Please, sir, I want some more.'

The master was a fat, healthy man; but he turned very pale. He gazed in stupefied astonishment on the small rebel for some seconds, and then clung for support to the copper. The assistants were paralysed with wonder; the boys with fear.

———

An excerpt from "Oliver Twist" by Charles Dickens

In the excerpt, the reader is aware of all the boys' feelings and beliefs. Therefore, the reader can make an informed opinion based on that knowledge.

Questions to consider:

1. What is the problem the boys face in the excerpt?
2. What did they ask Oliver Twist to do in the end?

PRACTICE EXERCISES

Read each passage below and answer the questions that follow.

PASSAGE 1

In a few days Mr. Bingley returned Mr. Bennet's visit, and sat about ten minutes with him in his library. He had entertained hopes of being admitted to a sight of the young ladies, of whose beauty he had heard much; but he saw only the father. The ladies were somewhat more fortunate, for they had the advantage of ascertaining from an upper window, that he wore a blue coat and rode a black horse.

An invitation to dinner was soon afterwards dispatched; and already had Mrs. Bennet planned the courses that were to do credit to her housekeeping, when an answer arrived which deferred it all. Mr. Bingley was obliged to be in town the following day, and consequently unable to accept the honour of their invitation, &c. Mrs. Bennet was quite disconcerted. She could not imagine what business he could have in town so soon after his arrival in Hertfordshire; and she began to fear that he might be always flying about from one place to another, and never settled at Netherfield as he ought to be. Lady Lucas quieted her fears a little by starting the idea of his being gone to London only to get a large party for the ball; and a report soon followed that Mr. Bingley was to bring twelve ladies and seven gentlemen with him to the assembly. The girls grieved over such a number of ladies; but were comforted the day before the ball by hearing, that instead of twelve, he had brought only six with him from London, his five sisters and a cousin. And when the party entered the assembly room, it consisted of only five altogether; Mr. Bingley, his two sisters, the husband of the eldest, and another young man.

Mr. Bingley was good looking and gentleman-like; he had a pleasant countenance, and easy, unaffected manners. His sisters were fine women, with an air of decided fashion. His brother-in-law, Mr. Hurst, merely looked the gentleman; but his friend Mr. Darcy soon drew the attention of the room by his fine, tall person, handsome features, noble mien; and the report which was in general circulation within five minutes after his entrance, of his having ten thousand a year. The gentlemen pronounced him to be a fine figure of a man, the ladies declared he was much handsomer than Mr. Bingley, and he was looked at with great admiration for about half the evening, till his manners gave a disgust which turned the tide of his popularity; for he was discovered to be proud, to be above his company, and above being pleased; and not all his large estate in Derbyshire could then save him from having a most forbidding, disagreeable countenance, and being unworthy to be compared with his friend.

An excerpt from "Pride and Prejudice" by Jane Austen

1. In what point of view is the passage written?

    a. First-person POV
    b. Second-person POV
    c. Limited third-person POV
    d. Omniscient third-person POV

2. Which choice best supports your answer for question 1?

    a. The narrator speaks about his hopes and dreams.
    b. The second-person pronoun is used.
    c. The reader has access to all the characters' thoughts and feelings, including Mr. Bingley's and Mrs. Bennet's.
    d. The reader only has access to Mr. Bingley's thoughts.

PASSAGE 2

No, when I go to sea, I go as a simple sailor, right before the mast, plumb down into the forecastle, aloft there to the royal mast-head. True, they rather order me about some, and make me jump from spar to spar, like a grasshopper in a May meadow. And at first, this sort of thing is unpleasant enough. It touches one's sense of honor, particularly if you come of an old established family in the land, the Van Rensselaers, or Randolphs, or Hardicanutes. And more than all, if just previous to putting your hand into the tar-pot, you have been lording it as a country schoolmaster, making the tallest boys stand in awe of you. The transition is a keen one, I assure you, from a schoolmaster to a sailor, and requires a strong decoction of Seneca and the Stoics to enable you to grin and bear it. But even this wears off in time.

What of it, if some old hunks of a sea-captain orders me to get a broom and sweep down the decks? What does that indignity amount to, weighed, I mean, in the scales of the New Testament? Do you think the archangel Gabriel thinks anything the less of me, because I promptly and respectfully obey that old hunks in that particular instance? Who ain't a slave? Tell me that. Well, then, however the old sea-captains may order me about—however they may thump and punch me about, I have the satisfaction of knowing that it is all right; that everybody else is one way or other served in much the same way— either in a physical or metaphysical point of view, that is; and so the universal thump is passed round, and all hands should rub each other's shoulder-blades, and be content.

Again, I always go to sea as a sailor, because they make a point of paying me for my trouble, whereas they never pay passengers a single penny that I ever heard of. On the contrary, passengers themselves must pay. And there is all the difference in the world between paying and being paid. The act of paying is perhaps the most uncomfortable infliction that the two orchard thieves entailed upon us. But being paid,— what will compare with it? The urbane activity with which a man receives money is really marvellous, considering that we so earnestly believe money to be the root of all earthly ills, and that on no account can a monied man enter heaven. Ah! how cheerfully we consign ourselves to perdition!

Excerpt from "Moby Dick" by Herman Melville

1. In what point of view is the passage written?

   a. First-person POV
   b. Second-person POV
   c. Limited third-person POV
   d. Omniscient third-person POV

2. Which choice best supports your answer for question 1?

   a. The first-person pronoun is used.
   b. The narrator speaks directly to the reader.
   c. The reader knows the sea-captain's thoughts.
   d. The reader has access to all characters' thoughts.

REFLECTION ON LEARNING

Answer the following reflection questions and feel free to discuss your responses with your teacher or a classmate.

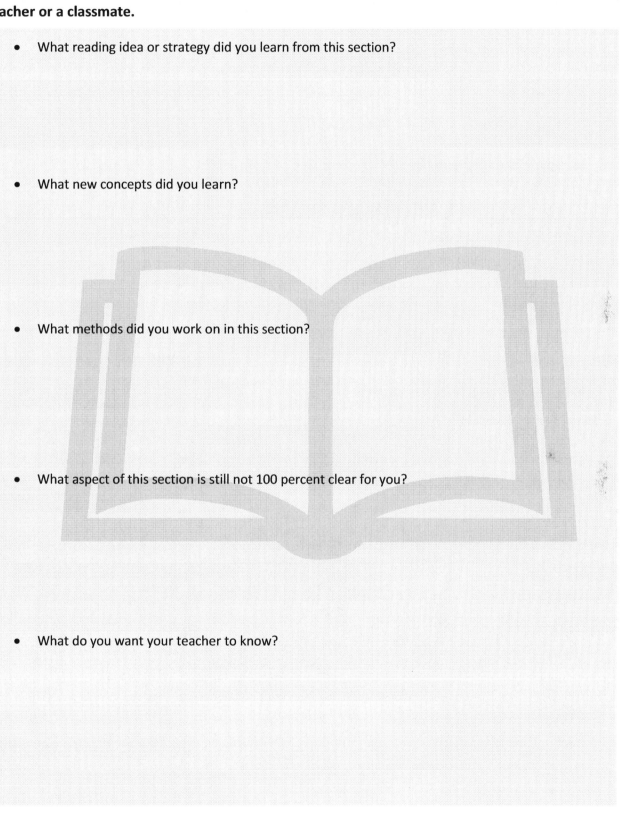

- What reading idea or strategy did you learn from this section?

- What new concepts did you learn?

- What methods did you work on in this section?

- What aspect of this section is still not 100 percent clear for you?

- What do you want your teacher to know?

LESSON 11
ANALYZING THE AUTHOR'S PURPOSE AND TECHNIQUE

In this lesson, you will learn to determine the author's purpose by analyzing the techniques they use.

The **author's purpose** is the reason they wrote the text. Here are some reasons for writing:

- To entertain
- To inform
- To persuade
- To express thoughts and feelings
- To arouse emotions and thoughts

One text may have several purposes that are revealed by the various techniques the writer uses. Here are some clues to help you determine the author's purpose.

1. **Overt statements**

Sometimes, an author would write an overt statement or openly state their purpose for writing a piece.

Example: *Coffee is a popular beverage that you may depend on to jumpstart your day. However, let me convince you to make the switch to its decaffeinated form.*

In this piece, the writer clearly states that she is attempting to convince the reader to switch from caffeinated coffee to decaffeinated. Therefore, the piece is persuasive.

2. **The basics**

Review the title, topic, illustrations and intended audience of the text. Additionally, pay attention to where the work is published. These can give an idea of the author's purpose.

Example: You see an article entitled "Tips for Communicating with Your Teenager" in the magazine, *A Parent's Guide to Teenagers*. You can conclude that the author's purpose is to inform parents of useful ways of communicating with their teenagers.

3. **Language use**

A writer may choose to be humorous to entertain the reader or sarcastic to express his displeasure over a particular issue. For this reason, it is important to look at the writer's **tone** and **word choices** when identifying the purpose. Are **negative**, **positive** or **neutral** words used?

Examples:

- **Neutral**: *According to the National Highway Traffic Safety Administration, 2,841 persons were killed due to distracted driving.*

   Purpose: To inform

- **Negative**: *The National Highway Traffic Safety Administration reports that an <u>alarming</u> number of persons (2,841) were <u>devastatingly</u> killed due to distracted driving.*

   Purpose: To persuade or express disapproval

Furthermore, determine if the writer uses **facts** or **opinions** in the text.

A **fact** is something that is known and proven to be true.

   Example: *Millions of bacteria live on human skin.* (This has been proven through the use of microscopes.)

An **opinion** is someone's belief or view on something. It is subjective and cannot be proven to be true.

   Example: *It is <u>disgusting</u> that millions of bacteria live on human skin.* (This is the writer's opinion and not everyone would agree since bacteria can't be seen with the naked eye.)

4. **Text structure**

Do you remember the types of text structure? The following are the main ones:

- Description
- Sequence or Chronology
- Cause and effect
- Compare and contrast
- Problem-solution

The text structure is a technique the writer uses to serve his or her purpose.

Example: *Fear gripped me and I stood frozen behind the door. I could hear the clumsy creature scuttling around outside and smell its putrid flesh. I prayed that it would not enter the room.*

In this example, the author chooses a descriptive text structure to describe his experience and feelings.

5. **Evidence and References**

Analyze the types of details the writer uses to support the main statements. Are there statistics, facts, observations, definitions, quotations and citations from other works? Or does the writer choose to appeal to the reader's emotions and experiences?

Example: *It is the pro bodybuilder and four-time Mr. Olympia, Jay Cutler, that said, "What hurts today makes you stronger tomorrow." So comrades, don't let the physical pain be a negative experience that thwarts your fitness journey.*

The example above gives a motivational quote from Jay Cutler, a bodybuilder and four-time Mr. Olympia. Therefore, the purpose of the piece is to motivate the reader to continue exercising.

Practice Exercise

Read the passage below and answer the following questions.

Buccaneers and Marooners of the Spanish Main

It is thence that the marooners took their name, for marooning was one of their most effective instruments of punishment or revenge. If a pirate broke one of the many rules which governed the particular band to which he belonged, he was marooned; did a captain defend his ship to such a degree as to be unpleasant to the pirates attacking it, he was marooned; even the pirate captain himself, if he displeased his followers by the severity of his rule, was in danger of having the same punishment visited upon him which he had perhaps more than once visited upon another.

The process of marooning was as simple as terrible. A suitable place was chosen (generally some desert isle as far removed as possible from the pathway of commerce), and the condemned man was rowed from the ship to the beach. Out he was bundled upon the sand spit; a gun, a half dozen bullets, a few pinches of powder, and a bottle of water were chucked ashore after him, and away rowed the boat's crew back to the ship, leaving the poor wretch alone to rave away his life in madness, or to sit sunken in his gloomy despair till death mercifully released him from torment. It rarely if ever happened that anything was known of him after having been marooned. A boat's crew from some vessel, sailing by chance that way, might perhaps find a few chalky bones bleaching upon the white sand in the garish glare of the sunlight, but that was all. And such were marooners.

By far the largest number of pirate captains were Englishmen, for, from the days of good Queen Bess, English sea captains seemed to have a natural turn for any species of venture that had a smack of piracy in it, and from the great Admiral Drake of the old, old days, to the truculent Morgan of buccaneering times, the Englishman did the boldest and wickedest deeds, and wrought the most damage.

First of all upon the list of pirates stands the bold Captain Avary, one of the institutors of marooning. Him we see but dimly, half hidden by the glamouring mists of legends and tradition. Others who came afterward outstripped him far enough in their doings, but he stands pre-eminent as the first of marooners of whom actual history has been handed down to us of the present day.

When the English, Dutch, and Spanish entered into an alliance to suppress buccaneering in the West Indies, certain worthies of Bristol, in old England, fitted out two vessels to assist in this laudable project; for doubtless Bristol trade suffered smartly from the Morgans and the l'Olonoises of that old time. One of these vessels was named the Duke, of which a certain Captain Gibson was the commander and Avary the mate.

Away they sailed to the West Indies, and there Avary became impressed by the advantages offered by piracy, and by the amount of good things that were to be gained by very little striving.

_____

An excerpt from *Howard Pyle's Book of Pirates* by Merle Johnson

1. The passage is mainly about what?

   a. The advantages of piracy
   b. The deeds of Captain Avary
   c. English sea captains
   d. The history of piracy

2. For what purpose did the writer most likely write this passage?

   a. To entertain the reader with exciting pirate stories
   b. To express his belief that piracy was horrific
   c. To inform the reader of pirates' rules
   d. To persuade the reader to become a pirate

3. The writer accomplishes his goal by using…

   a. words such as "terrible" and "wickedest" to describe piracy
   b. a humorous tone
   c. statistics and figures
   d. factual statements only

4. Explain what you understand by the term "marooning" as described in the passage.

   a. Choosing a deserted island to hide treasures attained after robberies
   b. Robbing and killing sailors and leaving their bodies on deserted islands
   c. Robbing and leaving victims on deserted islands
   d. The act of defending one's ship from pirates

5. Write some facts and opinions you found in the text.

FACTS	OPINIONS

REFLECTION ON LEARNING

Answer the following reflection questions and feel free to discuss your responses with your teacher or a classmate.

- What reading idea or strategy did you learn from this section?

- What new concepts did you learn?

- What methods did you work on in this section?

- What aspect of this section is still not 100 percent clear for you?

- What do you want your teacher to know?

LESSON 12
EVALUATING THE CREDIBILITY OF TEXTS

By the end of this lesson, you will be able to evaluate the credibility of non-fiction texts.

A text must be trustworthy and believable to be credible. Sources such as the Internet can contain information on almost any topic. While some information is accurate, some is false. As an active reader, it is essential to be able to distinguish between the two.

Here are some aspects of a text that you can analyze to determine its credibility.

1. **Author**

> **Ask yourself:**
> "Is the author an expert on the topic?"

Research and determine if the author is qualified and experienced enough to speak on the topic.

2. **Purpose**

> **Ask yourself:**
> "What is the purpose of the text?"

Use the clues available to identify the author's purpose for writing the text. In this way, you can decide if the writer has a hidden agenda to make you think, act or feel a particular way.

3. **Perspective**

> **Ask yourself:**
> "What is the author's point of view?"

Examine the content, word choice and tone of the writer to determine his point of view.

4. **Evidence and References**

> **Ask yourself:**
> "Is the text supported by valid evidence and references?"

Quotations, statistics, citations and other references and details should be from reputable persons, organizations and institutions, such as researchers, newspapers and government organizations.

5. **Relevance**

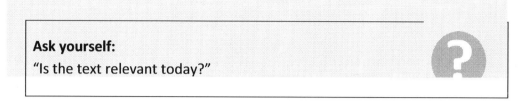

Ask yourself:
"Is the text relevant today?"

The publication date of the text can help you decide if the information is current.

6. **Prior know**

Ask yourself:

Use your prior knowledge to connect with the details being given. If you do not have enough prior knowledge to determine if the text is credible, you may want to seek other sources to cross-reference information in the text.

Now let's read the text below and evaluate its credibility.

ELEMENTS
OF
PLUMBING
BY
SAMUEL EDWARD DIBBLE

HEAD OF SANITARY EQUIPMENT AND INSTALLATION DEPT.
CARNEGIE INSTITUTE OF TECHNOLOGY

McGRAW-HILL BOOK COMPANY, Inc.
239 WEST 39TH STREET. NEW YORK

LONDON: HILL PUBLISHING CO., LTD.
6 & 8 BOUVERIE ST., E. C.
1918

CHAPTER I
PLUMBING FIXTURES AND TRADE

Modern plumbing as a trade is the arranging and running of pipes to supply pure water to buildings, the erecting of fixtures for the use of this supply, and the installing of other pipes for the resulting waste water. The work of the trade divides itself therefore into two parts: first the providing an adequate supply of water; and second, the disposing of this water after use. The first division offers few problems to the plumber, little variety in the layout being possible, and the result depending mostly upon the arrangement of the pipes and fittings; but the second division calls for careful study in the arrangement, good workmanship in the installing, and individual attention to each fixture.

The trade had its beginnings in merely supplying fresh water to a community. This was done by means of trenching, or conveying water from lakes, rivers, or springs through wooden pipes or open troughs. By easy stages the trade improved and enlarged its scope, until at the present time it is able to provide for the adequate distribution of tons of water under high pressure furnished by the city water works.

In the early years of the trade the question of the disposal of the waste water was easily answered, for it was allowed to be discharged onto the ground to seek its own course. But with the increased amount of water available, the waste-water problem has enlarged until today it plays the most important part of plumbing, and the trade has had to change to meet this waste-water problem.

The first simple system of a pipe running from the sink to a point outside the building was sufficient. As larger buildings came into use and communities were more thickly populated, the plumbing problem demanded thought and intense study. The waste pipes from fixtures had to be so arranged that it would be impossible for foul odors and germ-laden air to enter the building through a plumbing fixture. The importance of this is evidenced by the plumbing laws now in use throughout the country.

1. AUTHOR

It is stated that the author, Samuel Edward Dibble, is the Head Of Sanitary Equipment and Installation Dept., Carnegie Institute Of Technology. Therefore, he is qualified to speak on the topic of plumbing.

2. PURPOSE

The purpose is to inform the reader of the elements of plumbing.

3. PERSPECTIVE

The writer is objective and does not include any opinions in the excerpt.

4. EVIDENCE AND REFERENCES

The writer, who seems to be a credible source, does not make references in the excerpt. He writes using his expertise.

5. RELEVANCE

The text is dated 1918, which may not be considered current.

6. PRIOR KNOWLEDGE

You may have an idea of what plumbing entails and how plumbing systems look. You can then deduce that the writer's explanations and definitions align with the knowledge that you have.

CREDIBILITY

We can conclude that the text is credible as the author is an expert and his piece offers a basic explanation of what plumbing entails. Although the text was published in 1918, this explanation is still relevant today.

PRACTICE EXERCISES

Read the excerpt below.

ACROSS UNKNOWN SOUTH AMERICA
BY
A. HENRY SAVAGE-LANDOR

Printed in 1913
Copyright in the United States of America
by A. Henry Savage-Landor

This work is dedicated to the people of the great Brazilian Republic.

CHAPTER I

It would be impossible to enumerate here all the clever men of Brazil. They are indeed too numerous. The older generation has worked at great disadvantage owing to the difficulty of obtaining proper education. Many are the illiterate or almost illiterate people one finds even among the better classes. Now, however, excellent and most up-to-date schools have been established in the principal cities, and with the great enthusiasm and natural facility in learning of the younger generations wonderful results have been obtained. On account partly of the exhausting climate and the indolent life that Brazilians are inclined to lead, a good deal of the enthusiasm of youth dies out in later years; still Brazil has in its younger generation a great many men who are ambitious and heartily wish to render their country service. It is to be hoped that their efforts may be crowned with success. It is not talent which is lacking in Brazil, it is not patriotism; but persistence is not perhaps the chief characteristic among races of Portuguese descent. In these days of competition it is difficult to accomplish anything great without labour and trouble.

I left London on December 23rd, 1910, by the Royal Mail steamship Amazon, one of the most comfortable steamers I have ever been on.

We touched at Madeira, Pernambuco, and then at Bahia. Bahia seen from the sea was quite picturesque, with its two horizontal lines of buildings, one on the summit of a low hill-range, the other along the water line. A border of deep green vegetation separated the lower from the upper town. A massive red building stood prominent almost in the centre of the upper town, and also a number of church towers, the high dome of a church crowning the highest point.

I arrived in Rio de Janeiro on January 9th, 1911.

It is no use my giving a description of the city of Rio de Janeiro. Everybody knows that it is—from a pictorial point of view—quite a heavenly spot. Few seaside cities on earth can expect to have such a glorious background of fantastic mountains, and at the same time be situated on one of the most wonderful harbours known. I have personally seen a harbour which was quite as strangely interesting as the Rio harbour—but there was no city on it. It was the Malampaya Sound, on the Island of Palawan (Philippine Archipelago). But such an ensemble of Nature's wonderful work combined with man's cannot, to the best of my knowledge, be found anywhere else than in Rio.

1. What is most likely the author's purpose for writing the excerpt?

   a. To explain the culture of Brazil

   b. To record the events of his visit to Brazil

   c. To persuade the reader not to visit Brazil

   d. To entertain the reader with stories of Brazil

2. From which point of view is the piece written?

   a. The first-person point of view

   b. The second-person point of view

   c. The third-person limited point of view

   d. The third-person omniscient point of view

3. Which statement is true about the author?

   a. The author is writing from a subjective perspective and freely expresses his opinions.

   b. The author is objective and only states facts.

   c. The author is Brazilian and has first-hand experience of Brazil's culture.

   d. The author is not Brazilian and does not have first-hand experience of the country.

4. What technique does the author use to achieve his purpose?

   a. He uses using derogatory words and phrases.

   b. He states only facts such as dates and names of places.

   c. He describes his observations of Brazil's people and landscape.

   d. He uses valid and current references.

5. Is this a credible source for readers wishing to learn more about Brazil? Explain.

   _____

   _____

REFLECTION ON LEARNING

Answer the following reflection questions and feel free to discuss your responses with your teacher or a classmate.

- What reading idea or strategy did you learn from this section?

- What new concepts did you learn?

- What methods did you work on in this section?

- What aspect of this section is still not 100 percent clear for you?

- What do you want your teacher to know?

ASSESSMENT

READING PRACTICE TEST I

You will read multiple passages and answer 40 questions.
Your test time will be about 1 minute, 44 seconds per question.
Your total time for this test is one hour (60 minutes).

PASSAGE 1

ON PAROLE

I was wakened—indeed, we were all wakened, for I could see even the sentinel shake himself together from where he had fallen against the door-post—by a clear, hearty voice hailing us from the margin of the wood:

"Block house, ahoy!" it cried. "Here's the doctor."

And the doctor it was. Although I was glad to hear the sound, yet my gladness was not without admixture. I remembered with confusion my insubordinate and stealthy conduct, and when I saw where it had brought me—among what companions and surrounded by what dangers—I felt ashamed to look him in the face.

He must have risen in the dark, for the day had hardly come; and when I ran to a loophole and looked out, I saw him standing, like Silver once before, up to the mid-leg in creeping vapour.

"You, doctor! Top o' the morning to you, sir!" cried Silver, broad awake and beaming with good nature in a moment. "Bright and early, to be sure; and it's the early bird, as the saying goes, that gets the rations. George, shake up your timbers, son, and help Dr. Livesey over the ship's side. All a-doin' well, your patients was—all well and merry."

So he pattered on, standing on the hilltop with his crutch under his elbow and one hand upon the side of the log-house—quite the old John in voice, manner, and expression.

"We've quite a surprise for you too, sir," he continued. "We've a little stranger here—he! he! A noo boarder and lodger, sir, and looking fit and taut as a fiddle; slep' like a supercargo, he did, right alongside of John—stem to stem we was, all night."

Dr. Livesey was by this time across the stockade and pretty near the cook, and I could hear the alteration in his voice as he said, "Not Jim?"

"The very same Jim as ever was," says Silver.

The doctor stopped outright, although he did not speak, and it was some seconds before he seemed able to move on.

"Well, well," he said at last, "duty first and pleasure afterwards, as you might have said yourself, Silver. Let us overhaul these patients of yours."

A moment afterwards he had entered the block house and with one grim nod to me proceeded with his work among the sick. He seemed under no apprehension, though he must have known that his life, among these treacherous demons, depended on a hair; and he rattled on to his patients as if he were paying an ordinary professional visit in a quiet English family. His manner, I suppose, reacted on the men, for they behaved to him as if nothing had occurred, as if he were still ship's doctor and they still faithful hands before the mast.

———

An excerpt from Treasure Island by Robert Louis Stevenson

1. **PART A**
   Read this sentence from the passage:
   "He seemed under no <u>apprehension</u>, though he must have known that his life, among these treacherous demons, depended on a hair."

   Which word is the same as "**apprehension**?"

   a. Anger
   b. Unease
   c. Joy
   d. Boredom

2. Why does the narrator feel ashamed to see the doctor?

   a. He has betrayed the doctor in the past.

   b. He has forgotten the doctor is to visit.

   c. His friends have treated the doctor badly.

   d. He has not done what the doctor wished.

4. **PART A**
   Based on the details in the passage, what is the <u>best</u> description of the doctor's personality?

   a. Cowardly
   b. Moody
   c. Courageous
   d. Anxious

5. What does the narrator mean by the following line?

   "...yet my gladness was not without admixture."

   a. His gladness was overwhelming.
   b. He was glad but also angry.
   c. He felt confused about his gladness.
   d. He felt gladness, along with other emotions.

PART B
Which of the following clues <u>best</u> supports your answer to Part A?

a. The doctor is surrounded by terrible men but he still enjoys their company.
b. The doctor seems excited about the dangerous situation.
c. The doctor's life is in danger, but he is cool-headed rather than anxious.
d. Although his life is in danger, the doctor angrily refuses to help the men.

3. Which of the doctor's actions shows that he is wary of the men?

a. He had risen in the dark to attend to the men.
b. He rattled on to his patients as if he were paying an ordinary professional visit.
c. He was standing up to the mid-leg in creeping vapor.
d. He stopped and it was some seconds before he seemed able to move on.

PART B
Which of the following <u>best</u> provides evidence for the answer to Part A?

a. He treated the menacing men like a "quiet English family."
b. He awoke early.
c. He grimly nodded to the narrator.
d. He rattled his patients.

6. Identify the **two** similes used in the passage.

a. "looking fit and taut as a fiddle; slep' like a supercargo, he did"
b. "my insubordinate and stealthy conduct"
c. "a clear, hearty voice" and "the alteration in his voice"
d. "what companions and surrounded by what dangers"

7. Which of the following is an example of a metaphor?

a. "a clear, hearty voice hailing us"

b. "these treacherous demons"

c. "creeping vapour"

d. "we've a little stranger here"

8. From which point of view is the passage narrated?

a. 1st person

b. 2nd person

c. 3rd person limited

d. 3rd person omniscient

9. Think of the text clues, along with your background knowledge and world knowledge. What inference can you make about the passage?

a. The crew, including the narrator, had betrayed the doctor in some way.

b. The narrator alone betrayed the doctor.

c. The crew and doctor were loyal to each other.

d. The doctor had wronged the men.

10. Choose the title below that best captures the content of the passage.

a. The Doctor's Revenge

b. The Faithful Crewmen

c. The Doctor's Visit

d. The Good-Natured Silver

PASSAGE 2

THE BADGER

The badger is not by nature a ferocious animal, though the female will repel with the greatest savagery any approach when she has young, but so will a hen with chickens. The temperament of the badger is a gentle, shrinking one. No animal prefers a more quiet life, loving a warm bed in a dry dark corner of earth or rocks. He loves to sleep and meditate in peace for the greater part of the twenty-four hours. He lies not far within his entrance hall during the spring and summer, and on a hot day he will sometimes come to the mouth of his hole. In the evening, in June or July, he will come outside, sit looking into the wood or shuffle round the bushes, stretch himself against the tree-stems, or have a clumsy romp with his wife and little ones; and when the daylight dies he will hurry off, rushing through the covert for his nightly ramble. In the summer months he will travel as far as six miles from home, but he is in bed again an hour before sunrise.

It is only at this time of the year that he can be hunted above ground. This can be done with a few beagles or harriers on a moonlight night, when, finding him in the open, they will give a merry chase and fine cry, and a run of several miles without a check. If his earths are stopped, and he finds no other refuge, he will be brought to bay. In some districts I have known sacks put into the mouths of the most used holes of a set, the open end of each sack having a running noose pegged into the ground, thus providing an astonishing reception on his return as he charges in, disturbed or pursued in his midnight ramble. By this means he is taken alive and unhurt, being bagged and secured in his attempt to enter. At other times of the year, when the days are short and the nights longer, he comes out later in the evening, waits for a moment at the mouth of his earth, takes a preliminary sniff round, and then rushes off at the top speed into the covert.

The badger is easily domesticated if brought up by hand, and proves an interesting and charming companion. I had at one time two that I could do anything with and which followed me so closely that they would bump against my boots each step I took, and come and snuggle in under my coat when I sat down. I was very much attached to them, but having to leave for the London season, I came home after a prolonged absence to find that they had reverted to their natural disposition, and had forgotten him who had been a foster-parent to them. As I could not fondle them without a pair of hedging-gloves on, and they no longer walked at my heel, I made them a home in the woods, where the thought of their happiness has helped me to bear my loss.

———

An excerpt from "The Badger" by Alfred E. Pease

11. In which season can badgers be hunted above ground?

    a. Winter
    b. Spring
    c. Summer
    d. Fall

12. Which is the best description of the general nature of badgers?

    a. They are peaceful and quiet.
    b. They are aggressive and noisy.
    c. They are quiet but savage.
    d. They are noisy, playful and friendly.

13. Read this line from the passage:
"...the female will repel with the greatest savagery any approach when she has young, but so will a hen with chickens."

Why does the writer make this comparison?

a. To convince the reader that female badgers and chickens are aggressive
b. To show that badgers and chickens are gentle
c. To show that harmless animals can become aggressive when protecting their young
d. To show that badgers and chickens reproduce similarly

14. Read this sentence from the passage:
"The badger is easily domesticated if brought up by hand."

What is the meaning of the word "**domesticated**"?

a. To be bred for meat

b. To become miniature

c. To remain wild

d. To be tamed and kept as a pet

15. Where do badgers dwell?

a. In holes in the earth

b. In nests in trees

c. Among piles of rocks in grasslands

d. In clumps of bushes

16. What is the meaning of the following line?
"...they will give a merry chase and...a run of several miles without a check."

a. The animals will follow the badger although they get no reward.
b. The animals will persistently follow the badger without resting.
c. The animals will happily follow the badger without any reward.
d. The animals will chase the badger but will not hurt it.

17. **PART A**

Which of the following claims does the writer make in the passage?

a. Badgers are gentle, quiet animals.

b. Badgers are helpless, timid animals.

c. Badgers are ferocious animals.

d. Badgers can be lifelong companions.

PART B

Which of the following sentences is the best evidence against the writer's claim?

a. "The temperament of the badger is a gentle, shrinking one."
b. "He will travel as far as six miles from home."
c. "The female will repel with the greatest savagery any approach when she has young."
d. "The badger proves an interesting and charming companion."

18. **PART A**

What is the writer's <u>main</u> purpose in this passage?

a. To persuade
b. To inform
c. To entertain
d. To express

PART B

Which of the following <u>best</u> shows the writer's purpose?

a. He mostly expresses his fondness for badgers.
b. He recounts exciting tales of hunting badgers.
c. He urges the reader to keep badgers as pets.
d. He mostly describes the behavior of badgers.

19. What kind of evidence does the writer <u>mainly</u> use to support his view of badgers?

a. He uses experiences and opinions.
b. He uses facts backed up by references.
c. He uses statistics and figures.
d. He uses reasoning.

20. The writer states that "the thought of their happiness has helped me to bear my loss." What does this reveal about his feelings?

a. He selfishly wants to own badgers.
b. He despises badgers.
c. He is indifferent towards badgers.
d. He selflessly cares about badgers.

PASSAGE 3

THE PEOPLE AND THEIR INDUSTRIES

The process of pulping is simplicity itself; the trees are felled in the forests on the hillsides close by, and sawn into blocks. Aerial wires stretch from the felling ground to the works, and the blocks come swinging down in baskets, to be handed over forthwith to the mercy of the machinery. With the aid of heavy crushers and a certain amount of water the logs are soon reduced to pulp, which then floats away into sifters, to be eventually rolled out into flat sheets.

An immense amount of this pulp is exported to England in sacks, and is used for many other purposes besides paper-making.

Another thing which we get from Norway is ice. Most of those huge blocks of ice which you see in the fishmongers' shops in the summer have come across the North Sea, and ice-cutting is a very important business in the winter months. The ice is obtained principally from the mountain lakes, and in the vicinity of Christiania, long wooden chutes are erected from the mountain-tops to the edge of the fjord. Down these the huge cubes travel, direct from their homes to the deck of the boat, and thus save the cost of overland transport. They are sawn most carefully, the dimensions being about two feet each way; rope handles are then frozen into the blocks for facility of movement, and the cubes are stored in ice-houses until the summer, by which time they have lost almost half their original weight.

Next to timber, the chief export from the country is fish (including cod-liver oil). The great fisheries are round the Lofödden Islands on the North-West Coast, well within the Arctic Circle, and it is estimated that some 30,000 men and 6,000 boats are engaged in capturing the cod from January to April each year. The fishermen assemble from far and wide, and take up their residence for the season in temporary huts, clustered together on the shores of the islands. The work is arduous as well as dangerous, for storms and heavy seas are of frequent occurrence, and tides and currents among the islands most treacherous. And here, close to the fisheries, is situated the dreaded whirlpool, the Mælstrom of renown.

But it is the people's living, and in a favourable season they make immense hauls. An ordinary catch for an ordinary day is 500 cod per boat, and a good day will double that number, though in such a case the boat has to make a second trip to bring the fish ashore. A simple calculation will show that millions of cod are landed on the islands every day. Imagine the sight and imagine the smell!

An excerpt from "Peeps at Many Lands: Norway" by A.F. Mockler-Ferryman

PART A

21. What is the main idea of the passage?

a. Norway has many kinds of industries, including ice, timber and fish.
b. Norway exports different kinds of goods.
c. Exportation
d. It is easy to make a living in Norway.

22. Which paragraph describes the ice industry of Norway?

a. Paragraph 1
b. Paragraph 2
c. Paragraph 3
d. Paragraph 4

24. How is the cost of transport decreased in the ice-cutting industry?

a. Ice blocks are transported in baskets strung up by wire.
b. Ice blocks are transported via boat to the ice-houses.
c. Ice blocks float down the river and are gathered at the river's mouth.
d. Ice blocks are sent down the mountains through chutes.

26. **PART A**

Which of the statements is factual about the fishing industry in Norway?

a. It extends beyond the North-West Coast.
b. It is a seasonal industry.
c. It is a difficult but satisfying job.
d. It is a minor industry.

PART B

Choose a major supporting detail that best supports your answer to Part A.

a. The process of pulping is simple.
b. Fishing in Norway is dangerous.
c. Ice cutting is an important business.
d. An ordinary catch for a day is 500 cod per boat.

23. According to the passage, what is one use of the pulp exported to England?

a. It makes soap.
b. It produces paper.
c. It freezes fish.
d. It cuts ice.

25. Which of the following statements show the writer's opinion?

a. "Another thing which we get from Norway is ice."
b. "The process of pulping is simplicity itself."
c. "The ice is obtained principally from the mountain lakes…"
d. "…it is estimated that some 30,000 men and 6,000 boats are engaged…"

PART B

Which line is evidence of the answer to Part A?

a. The work is arduous as well as dangerous.
b. The great fisheries are around the Lofödden Islands.
c. Around 30,000 men and 6,000 boats are engaged each year.
d. The cod is captured from January to April each year.

27. What can one infer from these <u>two</u> facts on the fishing industry?
- Fishermen assemble from far and wide.
- The work is dangerous.

a. The industry is very profitable.
b. The work is not worth the trouble.
c. People dislike fishing.
d. Fishermen do not understand the risks of their job.

28. Read this sentence from the passage:
"The work is <u>arduous</u> as well as dangerous, for storms and heavy seas are of frequent occurrence..."

What is the meaning of the word "**arduous**?"

a. To be easily attainable
b. Occurring rarely
c. To require a great deal of effort
d. To be disloyal

29. What kind of evidence does the writer use to support his points?

a. He uses his opinion and experiences.
b. He uses only factual information.
c. He uses only statistics and figures.
d. He uses his opinion as well as factual information.

30. Think of the text clues, along with your background knowledge and world knowledge.

What inference can you make about Norway?

a. It consists mostly of flat land.
b. The climate is freezing cold, even during the summer.
c. It is a mountainous, temperate country.
d. It is a temperate country with mostly flat land.

PASSAGE 4

SENSUAL INDULGENCE AS A DUTY

Too long we have been allowing covetous manufacturers and dealers and incompetent or indolent cooks to spoil our naturally good food. We have done this because we have not as a nation understood that there is nothing in the world on which our health and hourly comfort, our happiness and our capacity for hard work, depend so much as on the Flavor of food—those savory qualities which make it appetizing and enjoyable and therefore digestible and helpful.

It is not too much to say that *the most important problem now before the American public is to learn to enjoy the pleasures of the table and to insist on having savory food at every meal.*

There was a time when it would have been considered rank heresy to express such an opinion, and even today there are millions of honest folk who hold that the enjoyment of a good meal is merely a form of sybaritic indulgence.

When Ruskin wrote his "Modern Painters" he referred to the indulgence of taste as an "ignoble source of pleasure." He lived to realize the foolishness of this sneer; in one of those amusing footnotes which he contributed to the final edition of that great work, and in which he often assails his own former opinions with merciless severity, he denounces the "cruelty and absurdity" of his failing to learn to appreciate the dainties provided by his father. But his earlier opinion reflected the general attitude of the time toward the pleasures of the table.

Fortunately, in our efforts to fight the great American plague—dyspepsia—we are no longer seriously hampered by that Puritan severity which caused the father of Walter Scott, when young Walter one day expressed his enjoyment of the soup, to promptly mix with it a pint of water to take the devil out of it.

America's leading educator, Ex-President Eliot of Harvard, has expressed the more rational view of our time in these words: "Sensuous pleasures, like eating and drinking, are sometimes described as animal, and therefore unworthy, but men are animals and have a right to enjoy without reproach those pleasures of animal existence which maintain health, strength, and life itself."

We may go farther than that, asserting that not only have we a right to enjoy the pleasures of the table, but it is our moral duty to do so. *The highest laws of health demand of us that we get as much pleasure out of our meals as possible.* To prove this statement is the main object of the present volume, nearly every page of which bears witness to its truth, directly or indirectly.

———

An excerpt from *Food and Flavor: A Gastronomic Guide to Health and Good Living* by Henry T. Finck

31. What is the <u>main</u> purpose of the passage?

a. To entertain the reader with interesting stories of eating unsavory foods

b. To inform the reader of the benefits of eating certain foods

c. To persuade the reader that savory foods are beneficial to one's health

d. To express his opinion on popular dishes

32. Read the line from the passage:
"...even today there are millions of honest folk who hold that the enjoyment of a good meal is merely a form of <u>sybaritic indulgence</u>."

What is your understanding of the phrase **"sybaritic indulgence?"**

a. Excessive gratification

b. Dissatisfaction

c. Laziness

d. Distastefulness

33. According to the writer, what is the relationship between savory foods and our health?

a. Eating savory foods leads to ill health.

b. Eating savory foods leads to good health.

c. Savory foods do not affect health.

d. Savory foods can sometimes be detrimental to health.

34. Read the following sentence from the article:
"Too long we have been allowing ... incompetent or <u>indolent</u> cooks to spoil our naturally good food. What is an antonym for the word **"indolent?"**

a. Determined

b. Lazy

c. Competitive

d. Hard-working

35. **PART A**

Read this sentence from the passage:

"...he often <u>assails</u> his own former opinions with merciless severity, he denounces the 'cruelty and absurdity' of his failing to learn to appreciate the dainties provided by his father."
What is a synonym for the word **"assails?"**

a. Compliments
b. Imagines
c. Criticizes
d. Appreciates

PART B

What type of context clue does the writer provide?

a. Synonym clue

b. Antonym clue

c. Definition clue

d. Explanation or example clue

36. The phrase, "pleasures of the table" is an example of...

a. Theme

b. Personification

c. A simile

d. A metaphor

37. The writer is <u>mainly</u> addressing whom in this article?

a. Humanity

b. Europeans

c. People of the Western Hemisphere

d. Americans

38. When Walter expressed his enjoyment of the soup, his father added water to it "to take the devil out of it."

Which sentence below would be the best inference of the situation?

a. His father preferred watery soup.

b. The taste of food was irrelevant.

c. It was considered wrongful to enjoy food.

d. Persons believed that the devil lived in soup.

39. What is the meaning of the underlined phrase in the third paragraph of the passage?

"...it would have been considered <u>rankheresy</u> to express such an opinion..."

a. Revolting and against what is acceptable

b. Normal and acceptable

c. Illegal

d. Admirable

40. **PART A**

In this article, the writer argues <u>against</u> a popular view. What is the view?

a. Flavorful foods are beneficial to our health.

b. It is disgraceful to enjoy flavorful foods.

c. Flavorful foods should only be consumed on special occasions.

d. It is encouraged to create flavorful foods.

PART B

He supports his belief by...

a. Using quotations and examples from reputable persons.

b. Using figures and statistics.

c. Using only factual information.

d. Using quotations and statistics.

ASSESSMENT

READING PRACTICE TEST II

You will read multiple passages and answer 40 questions.
Your test time will be about 1 minute, 44 seconds per question.
Your total time for this test is one hour (60 minutes).

PASSAGE 1

My father's family name being Pirrip, and my Christian name Philip, my infant tongue could make of both names nothing longer or more explicit than Pip. So, I called myself Pip, and came to be called Pip.

I give Pirrip as my father's family name, on the authority of his tombstone and my sister,—Mrs. Joe Gargery, who married the blacksmith. As I never saw my father or my mother, and never saw any likeness of either of them (for their days were long before the days of photographs), my first fancies regarding what they were like were unreasonably derived from their tombstones. The shape of the letters on my father's, gave me an odd idea that he was a square, stout, dark man, with curly black hair. From the character and turn of the inscription, "Also Georgiana Wife of the Above," I drew a childish conclusion that my mother was freckled and sickly. To five little stone lozenges, each about a foot and a half long, which were arranged in a neat row beside their grave, and were sacred to the memory of five little brothers of mine,—who gave up trying to get a living, exceedingly early in that universal struggle,—I am indebted for a belief I religiously entertained that they had all been born on their backs with their hands in their trousers-pockets, and had never taken them out in this state of existence.

Ours was the marsh country, down by the river, within, as the river wound, twenty miles of the sea. My first most vivid and broad impression of the identity of things seems to me to have been gained on a memorable raw afternoon towards evening. At such a time I found out for certain that this bleak place overgrown with nettles was the churchyard; and that Philip Pirrip, late of this parish, and also Georgiana wife of the above, were dead and buried; and that Alexander, Bartholomew, Abraham, Tobias, and Roger, infant children of the aforesaid, were also dead and buried; and that the dark flat wilderness beyond the churchyard, intersected with dikes and mounds and gates, with scattered cattle feeding on it, was the marshes; and that the low leaden line beyond was the river; and that the distant savage lair from which the wind was rushing was the sea; and that the small bundle of shivers growing afraid of it all and beginning to cry, was Pip.

———

An excerpt from "Great Expectations" by Charles Dickens

1. Why did the narrator call himself "Pip?"

a. It was the name on his birth certificate.
b. Everyone in the village called him this.
c. It was the only way he could pronounce his name as a child.
d. It was his beloved father's name.

2. How did the narrator find out that his father's surname was "Pirrip?"

a. From the hospital's records
b. From his father's tombstone
c. From descriptions written on his father's photographs
d. The narrator made up the surname.

3. According to the narrator, why didn't he know how his parents looked?

a. They were too poor to be painted or photographed.
b. Photography was not invented yet.
c. All paintings and photographs of them were destroyed.
d. His sister had hidden their photographs from him.

5. "...my infant tongue could make of both names nothing longer or more explicit than Pip."

What is the figurative device being used in this line of the passage?

a. Simile
b. Metaphor
c. Personification
d. Irony

4. Read the following line from the passage:

"...my first fancies regarding what they were like were <u>unreasonably derived</u> from their tombstones."

What is the meaning of "**unreasonably derived**?"

a. His impressions were irrationally based on his parents' tombstones.
b. His impressions were rationally based on his parents' tombstones.
c. The narrator spent a lot of time in front of his parents' tombstones.
d. He only thought of his parents when he visited their tombstones.

6. **Part A**

From what point of view is the narrator speaking?

a. First-person point of view
b. Second-person point of view
c. Third-person point of view, limited
d. Third-person point of view, omniscient

Part B

Which of the following gives the <u>best</u> evidence for the answer to Part A?

a. The narrator is writing an account of his past.
b. The writer uses the first-person pronouns.
c. The narrator's view is limited to one character.
d. The writer uses the second-person pronouns.

7. **PART A**

What is the mood of the passage?

a. Humorous

b. Gloomy

c. Peaceful

d. Ironic

PART B

Which line gives evidence for your answer to Part A?

a. "Ours was the marsh country, down by the river…"

b. "I religiously entertained that they had all been born on their backs with their hands in their trousers-pockets…"

c. "So, I called myself Pip, and came to be called Pip."

d. "…the small bundle of shivers growing afraid of it all and beginning to cry, was Pip."

8. Pip begins to cry in the last line of the passage.

Which of the following answers is the best inference for his emotional reaction?

a. He feels lonely and afraid of the bleak country.

b. He is overcome with joy.

c. He is terrified that ghosts will haunt him.

d. His father had just died.

9. Read the last paragraph that begins, "ours was the marsh country…"

Which of the following sense images is mainly used in the paragraph?

a. Taste

b. Smell

c. Hearing

d. Sight

10. Choose the title that best captures the content of this passage.

a. Phillip Pirrip

b. A New Beginning

c. My Departed Family

d. The Bleak Marshes

PASSAGE 2

ALL ABOUT OWLS

The owl kills small birds, large insects, frogs and even fishes, but these are extras: its profession is rat-catching and mousing, and only those who have a very intimate personal acquaintance with it know how peculiarly its equipment and methods are adapted to this work. The falcon gives open chase to the wild duck, keeping above it if possible until near enough for a last spurt; then it comes down at a speed which is terrific, and, striking the duck from above, dashes it to the ground. The sparrow hawk plunges unexpectedly into a group of little birds and nips up one with a long outstretched foot before they have time to get clear of each other. The harrier skims over field, copse and meadow, suddenly rounding corners and topping fences and surprising small birds, or mice, on which it drops before they have recovered from their surprise.

The owl does none of these things. For one thing, it hunts in the night, when its sight is keenest and rats are abroad feeding. Its flight is almost noiseless and yet marvelously light and rapid when it pleases. Sailing over field, lane and hedgerow and examining the ground as it goes, it finds a likely place and takes a post of observation on a fence perhaps, or a sheaf of corn. Here it sits, bolt upright, all eyes. It sees a rat emerge from the grass and advance slowly, as it feeds, into open ground. There is no hurry, for the doom of that rat is already fixed. So the owl just sits and watches till the right moment has arrived; then it flits swiftly, softly, silently, across the intervening space and drops like a flake of snow. Without warning, or suspicion of danger, the rat feels eight sharp claws buried in its flesh. It protests with frantic squeals, but these are stopped with a nip that crunches its skull, and the owl is away with it to the old tower, where the hungry children are calling, with weird, impatient hisses, for something to eat.

The owl does not hunt the fields and hedgerows only. It goes to all places where rats or mice may be, reconnoiters farmyards, barns and dwelling houses and boldly enters open windows. Sometimes it hovers in the air, like a kestrel, scanning the ground below. And though its regular hunting hours are from dusk till dawn, it has been seen at work as late as nine or ten on a bright summer morning. But the vulgar boys of bird society are fond of mobbing it when it appears abroad by day, and it dislikes publicity.

An excerpt from *Concerning Animals and Other Matters* by E.H. Aitken

11. What does the writer mean by "its profession is rat-catching and mousing?"

a. The owl is trained to catch rats and mice for people.
b. The owl engages in setting traps for rats and mice.
c. The owl's main way of surviving is hunting and feeding on rats and mice.
d. The owl catches rats and mice when there's no other prey available.

12. According to the passage, what "equipment and methods" does the owl use to catch its prey?

a. It waits for the right moment to swiftly swoop down and grab its prey.
b. It gives an open chase to its prey.
c. It plunges unexpectedly into groups of prey.
d. It tricks its prey into being caught.

13. Why did the writer compare owls with falcons, sparrow hawks and harriers?

   a. He wanted to show that owls are similar to many other birds.
   b. He wanted to emphasize that owls use unique hunting methods.
   c. He wanted the reader to recognize the differences in their physical characteristics.
   d. He was showing the similarities in the birds' diets.

14. " But the vulgar boys of bird society are fond of mobbing it when it appears abroad by day…"

What can one infer about the writer's views of birds other than owls?

   a. He views their aggressive behavior as similar to owls'.
   b. He thinks they are pleasant, serene animals.
   c. He believes they are rightfully aggressive to other animals.
   d. He views them as being rude.

15. **PART A**

How does the narrator feel about owls?

   a. He is indifferent towards them.
   b. He despises them.
   c. He admires them.
   d. He has mixed feelings about them.

PART B

Which line gives evidence for your answer to Part A?

   a. "The owl does not hunt the fields and hedgerows only."
   b. "Its flight is almost noiseless and yet marvelously light and rapid when it pleases."
   c. "…the owl is away with it to the old tower…"
   d. "…it has been seen at work as late as nine or ten…"

16. Read the following line from the passage:

"…it flits swiftly, softly, silently, across the intervening space and drops like a flake of snow."

What figurative device is used?

   a. Simile
   b. Metaphor
   c. Personification
   d. Irony

17. **PART A**

According to the writer, which statement is <u>true</u> about owls?

   a. They always capture their prey.
   b. They are heavy and tough.
   c. They are opportunist hunters.
   d. They only feed in the night.

PART B

Which of the following lines from the passage is the best evidence of the statement?

   a. "…its profession is rat-catching and mousing."
   b. "It goes to all places where rats or mice may be…"
   c. "There is no hurry, for the doom of that rat is already fixed."
   d. "…it finds a likely place and takes a post of observation…"

18. What is the writer's purpose for writing this passage?

    a. To express

    b. To persuade

    c. To entertain

    d. To inform

20. Which technique does the writer <u>mainly</u> use in the passage?

    a. Compare and contrast

    b. Problem-solution

    c. Sequence or chronology

    d. Description

19. Which is the best summary of the passage?

    a. Owls are successful hunters that also may hunt other birds such as falcons, sparrow hawks and harrier. They mainly hunt at night using a unique method.

    b. Owls mainly hunt small prey, particularly rats and mice. They usually hunt at night using a unique hunting technique.

    c. Owls are similar to falcons, sparrow hawks and harrier. They all hunt small prey and are active at night.

    d. Owls hunt by plunging unexpectedly into groups of prey. They hunt mainly from dusk until dawn.

PASSAGE 3

THE DANCE FESTIVALS

The Dance Festivals of the Alaskan Eskimo are held during that cold, stormy period of the winter when the work of the year is over and hunting is temporarily at an end. At this season the people gather in the kásgi to celebrate the local rites, and at certain intervals invite neighboring tribes to join in the great inter-tribal festivals. This season of mirth and song is termed "Tcauyávik" the drum dance season, from "Tcaúyak" meaning drum. It lasts from November to March, and is a continuous succession of feasts and dances, which makes glad the heart of the Eskimo and serves to lighten the natural depression caused by day after day of interminable wind and darkness. A brisk exchange of presents at the local festivals promotes good feeling, and an interchange of commodities between the tribes at the great feasts stimulates trade and results in each being supplied with the necessities of life. For instance, northern tribes visiting the south bring presents of reindeer skins or múkluk to eke out the scanty supply of the south, while the latter in return give their visitors loads of dried salmon which the northerners feed to their dogs.

The festivals also serve to keep alive the religious feeling of the people, as evidenced in the Dance to the Dead, which allows free play to the nobler sentiments of filial faith and paternal love. The recital of the deeds of ancient heroes preserves the best traditions of the race and inspires the younger generation. To my mind, there is nothing which civilization can supply which can take the place of the healthy exercise, social enjoyment, commercial advantages, and spiritual uplift of these dances. Where missionary sentiment is overwhelming they are gradually being abandoned; where there is a mistaken opinion in regard to their use, they have been given up altogether; but the tenacity with which the Eskimo clings to these ancient observances, even in places where they have been nominal Christians for years, is an evidence of the vitality of these ancient rites and their adaptation to the native mind.

The festivals vary considerably according to locality, but their essential features are the same.

_____

An excerpt from "The Dance Festivals of the Alaskan Eskimo" by E.H. Hawkes

21. Why do the dance festivals take place during the winter?

a. Dancing is done to keep participants warm during the winter.
b. There is not much work being done, so people have time for festivals.
c. Winter is a lovely setting for festivals.
d. Winter marks the beginning of the Alaskan Eskimo calendar.

22. Which of the following is <u>not</u> stated in the passage as a purpose of the dance festivals?

a. They encourage inter-tribal interaction.
b. They improve the mood of the people during the dreary winter season.
c. They celebrate a new beginning to life.
d. They keep religious feelings alive.

23. **PART A**

Which statement is <u>factual</u> about the participants of these dances?

a. They may belong to different tribes.
b. They must each perform a ritual before participating.
c. They wear specially adorned costumes for the festival.
d. They give gifts that are uncommon in their land.

PART B

Choose the statement from the passage that gives the best evidence for your answer to Part A.

a. "...the people gather in the kásgi to celebrate the local rites..."
b. "...northern tribes visiting the south bring presents of reindeer skins or mukluk..."
c. "...at certain intervals invite neighboring tribes to join in the great inter-tribal festivals..."
d. "A brisk exchange of presents at the local festivals promotes good feeling..."

24. Which of the following activities take place at the dance festivals?

a. Dancing, drumming, exchanging gifts
b. Hunting, eating, trading
c. Exchanging gifts, drumming, hunting
d. Dancing, exchanging gifts, horseback riding

25. What is happening in the picture accompanying the passage?

a. Gifts are being exchanged.
b. Tribes are trading items.
c. Participants are eating.
d. People are playing the drums.

26. **PART A**

What is the writer's opinion on these festivals?

a. He does not express his opinion.
b. He believes they are frivolous forms of entertainment.
c. He thinks they are outdated.
d. He thinks they are beneficial and essential to humanity.

PART B

Which line from the passage <u>best</u> gives evidence for your answer to Part A?

a. "This season of mirth and song is termed 'Tcauyávik'..."
b. "To my mind, there is nothing which civilization can supply which can take the place...of these dances."
c. "Where missionary sentiment is overwhelming they are gradually being abandoned..."
d. "The festivals vary considerably..."

27. According to the passage, what is a <u>major</u> advantage of having inter-tribal festivals?

a.   People can have access to necessities by trading with other tribes.

b.   One can meet different people.

c.   One can learn about others' cultures.

d.   Participants can exchange gifts.

28. What does the following line infer?

"...where there is a mistaken opinion in regard to their use, they have been given up altogether."

a.   The Alaska Eskimos keep the truth about their festival a secret.
b.   The festival is so important that any false information is erased.
c.   Outsiders have given up on seeking the truth about the festival's purpose.
d.   Outsiders always spread false information on the festival.

29. Read the following line from the passage:

"...the <u>tenacity</u> with which the Eskimo clings to these ancient observances...is an evidence of the vitality of these ancient rites and their adaptation to the native mind..."

What is the meaning of the word "**tenacity**?"

a.   Carelessness
b.   Idleness
c.   Persistence
d.   Productivity

30. Which is the best summary of the passage?

a.   The dance festivals of the Alaskan Eskimos take place during the winter. They are essential for commercial, spiritual and social purposes.
b.   The dance festivals of the Alaskan Eskimos are beneficial.
c.   The dance festivals of the Alaskan Eskimos
d.   The festivals vary considerably according to the locality, but their essential features are the same.

PASSAGE 4

INTRODUCTION OF COFFEE INTO NORTH AMERICA

Undoubtedly the first to bring a knowledge of coffee to North America was Captain John Smith, who founded the Colony of Virginia at Jamestown in 1607. Captain Smith became familiar with coffee in his travels in Turkey.

Although the Dutch also had early knowledge of coffee, it does not appear that the Dutch West India Company brought any of it to the first permanent settlement on Manhattan Island (1624). Nor is there any record of coffee in the cargo of the Mayflower (1620), although it included a wooden mortar and pestle, later used to make "coffee powder."

In the period when New York was New Amsterdam, and under Dutch occupancy (1624–64), it is possible that coffee may have been imported from Holland, where it was being sold on the Amsterdam market as early as 1640, and where regular supplies of the green bean were being received from Mocha in 1663; but positive proof is lacking. The Dutch appear to have brought tea across the Atlantic from Holland before coffee. The English may have introduced the coffee drink into the New York colony between 1664 and 1673. The earliest reference to coffee in America is 1668, at which time a beverage made from the roasted beans, and flavored with sugar or honey, and cinnamon, was being drunk in New York.

Coffee first appears in the official records of the New England colony in 1670. In 1683, the year following William Penn's settlement on the Delaware, we find him buying supplies of coffee in the New York market and paying for them at the rate of eighteen shillings and nine pence per pound. Coffee houses patterned after the English and Continental prototypes were soon established in all the colonies.

Norfolk, Chicago, St. Louis, and New Orleans also had them. Conrad Leonhard's coffee house at 320 Market Street, St. Louis, was famous for its coffee and coffee cake, from 1844 to 1905, when it became a bakery and lunch room, removing in 1919 to Eighth and Pine Streets.

In the pioneer days of the great west, coffee and tea were hard to get; and, instead of them, teas were often made from garden herbs, spicewood, sassafras-roots, and other shrubs, taken from the thickets. In 1839, in the city of Chicago, one of the minor taverns was known as the Lake Street coffee house. It was situated at the corner of Lake and Wells Streets. A number of hotels, which in the English sense might more appropriately be called inns, met a demand for modest accommodation. Two coffee houses were listed in the Chicago directories for 1843 and 1845, the Washington coffee house, 83 Lake Street; and the Exchange coffee house, Clarke Street between La Salle and South Water Streets.

_____
An excerpt from *All About Coffee* by William H. Ukers

31. What is the <u>precise topic</u> of the passage?

    a. Coffee and coffee houses
    b. A history of beverages in North America
    c. Coffee was introduced to North America by Captain John Smith.
    d. The origin of coffee in North America

32. What kind of text structure does the writer <u>mainly</u> use in the passage?

    a. Description
    b. Sequence/ chronology
    c. Cause and effect
    d. Compare and contrast

33. **PART A**

Which country does the writer believe introduced coffee to North America?

    a. Holland
    b. England
    c. China
    d. Turkey

PART B

Which sentence from the passage is the <u>best</u> evidence for your answer to Part A?

    a. "The earliest reference to coffee in America is 1668."
    b. "The first to bring a knowledge of coffee…was Captain John Smith."
    c. "The English may have introduced the coffee drink."
    d. "The Dutch appear to have brought tea across the Atlantic…"

34. When was coffee first officially recorded in North America?

    a. 1670
    b. 1607
    c. 1620
    d. 1683

35. **PART A**

Using text clues and your world knowledge, how was it possible for coffee to be first made available to North America?

    a. It was brought by train.
    b. It was produced in home gardens.
    c. It was imported by plane.
    d. It was imported by ship.

PART B

Which of the following is the <u>best</u> evidence for your answer to Part A?

    a. The writer refers to the possibility that coffee was transported in the cargo of the Mayflower.
    b. Captain Smith learned about coffee from his travels in Turkey.
    c. William Penn bought coffee in the New York market.
    d. Teas were often made from garden herbs.

36. What was the writer's purpose in this reading?

    a. To inform
    b. To persuade
    c. To explain
    d. To entertain

37. According to the writer, why wasn't coffee used much during the pioneer days?

    a. Its popularity was in decline.
    b. It was thought to be poisonous.
    c. It was difficult to obtain.
    d. Workers on coffee estates were protesting.

38. Why do you think it is difficult for the writer to state <u>exactly</u> when and how coffee was first brought to North America?

    a.   The writer is unable to access any records.
    b.   Any official record of the event is most likely lost.
    c.   The writer is not interested in examining official records.
    d.   The writer is incapable of interpreting the historical documents.

40. Which of the following is the best summary of the article?

    a.   Coffee was first imported to North America by the English between 1664 and 1673. It became popular and led to the opening of various coffee houses.
    b.   Coffee was first imported by the Dutch during their occupancy in North America. It became popular, and many coffee houses were built as a result.
    c.   After it was brought to North America, coffee became difficult to obtain, and many coffee houses became bankrupt.
    d.   After Captain John Smith brought coffee to North America in 1607, the drink became so popular that the demand was soon higher than the supply.

39. Read the following sentence from the passage:

"Coffee houses patterned after the English and Continental <u>prototypes</u> were soon established in all the colonies."

What is the meaning of the word "**prototypes**" as used in the sentence?

    a.   Wooden structures
    b.   Hotels
    c.   New buildings
    d.   The first models or examples

REFLECTION ON LEARNING

Answer the following reflection questions and feel free to discuss your responses with your teacher or a classmate.

- How do you feel about your performance on the practice tests?

- Was anything too hard for you? What was it?

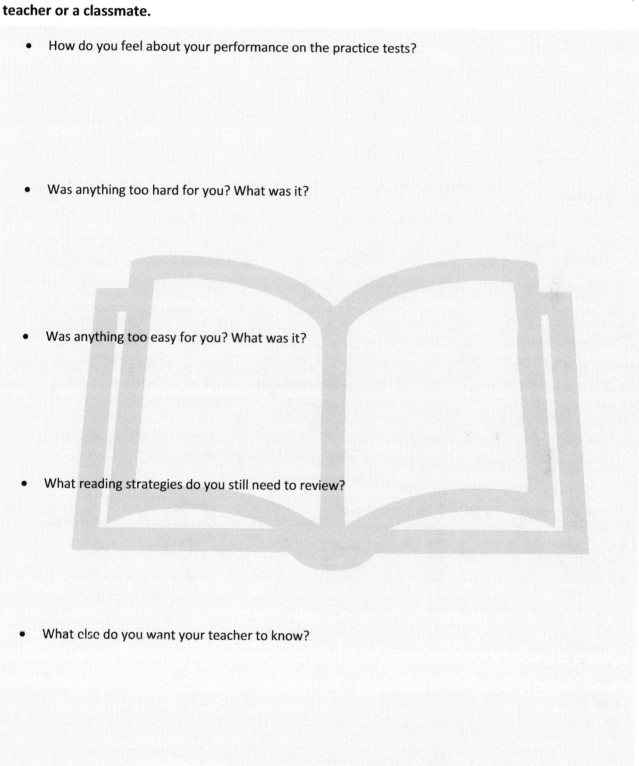

- Was anything too easy for you? What was it?

- What reading strategies do you still need to review?

- What else do you want your teacher to know?

ANSWER KEYS FOR THE PRACTICE EXERCISES

LESSON 1
Practice Exercises

1. b	3. a
2. d	4. c

Practice Exercises
Excerpt 1
d

Excerpt 2
b
Clue: synonym

Excerpt 3
1. d
2. b

LESSON 2
Practice Exercise

TEXT-TO-SELF	TEXT-TO-TEXT	TEXT-TO-WORLD
Does the text remind you of a personal experience? Yes, it reminds me of a dog fight I once witnessed.	**Does the passage remind you of any other text you've read?** *White Fang* by Jack London	**To what world events does the text relate?** The text can be compared to criminal gangs that fight for territory and respect.
Is the text different from your life? Yes. It is different as it describes dogs and their behaviors.	**Is the text different from texts that you've read?** Yes. I mostly read texts that are written about human nature and from human perspectives.	**Are the events in the passage different from events that happen in the world?** No, it correctly describes what happens in nature when animals fight ferociously for food and territory.

LESSON 3
Practice Exercises

Passage 1	Passage 2
1. b	1. a
2. d	2. c
3. a	3. a

LESSON 4
Practice Exercises
Passage 1
1. c
2. b
3. a
4. d
5. c

Passage 2
Summary: The Temperance Movement aimed to reduce the consumption of alcohol. First, the movement promoted drinking in moderation, then it encouraged persons to resist the temptation to drink. Its later goal was the banning of selling alcohol. The movement was largely associated with women and women became more involved in leadership positions with establishment of the Woman's Christian Temperance Union (WCTU).

LESSON 5
Scenario 3
What do you know? There are toys inside the flowerpot and a woman opens the door while holding a baby bottle.
What do you infer? The woman is caring for at least one child. She may have a child who placed the toys in the pot and a baby who she was feeding with the bottle.

Picture 3
What do you infer? The woman is looking for a spot to camp outdoors.

Picture 4
What do you know? The man in the picture is wearing attire similar to a firefighter's and he is using a fire hose.
What do you infer? The man is a firefighter who is extinguishing a fire.

Picture 5
What do you know? People sell food by displaying them in glass cases. The food in the picture looks like baked goods. Children like treats and there are two children eagerly looking at the display.
What do you infer? The children are buying treats from a food place.

Passage 3
Context clues
A man is operating a machine. The passage states that cotton gin made cotton very profitable, it increased cotton production, and modern versions of the cotton gin are still in use today.

Prior Knowledge: Cotton seeds were manually separated from the fibers and this was a time-consuming process.

Inference: The cotton gin is a machine used to quickly separate the seeds from the cotton fibers.

Passage 4

1. b
2. d
3. a
4. b
5. d

Picture
Context clues: The picture is of a car possibly from the 1930s or 40s. The people are also dressed in attire common around that era. The front left tire of the car is missing.

Prior knowledge: Sometimes, cars malfunction and wheels may become deflated or fall out if wheel nuts are not tightened enough.

Inference: A wheel of the car has fallen out and caused the car to off-balance and bend the wheel on the other side.

LESSON 7
Practice Exercises
Passage

1. c
2. b
3. a

Picture

1. a
2. d
3. c

LESSON 8

Sequence or Chronology

1. The leaves are dried in the air for a short time.	→	2. They are exposed to artificial heat.

The leaves are dried by fire.	←	The leaves are rolled up into balls, and their juices are squeezed out.

MAIN IDEA
To make green tea, the juices of the leaves are squeezed out and the leaves are dried without delay.

Compare and Contrast

MAIN IDEA	
Abraham Lincoln and Frederick Douglass were ambitious and compassionate men who overcame poverty to fight for freedom and equality for all.	

SIMILARITIES	DIFFERENCES
• They were both poor. • They were advocates for freedom and equality.	• Lincoln was born to poor farmers while Douglass was born into slavery. • Lincoln was born in Kentucky while Douglass was from Maryland. • Lincoln earned a law degree and was elected to national-level office. Douglass did not have such formal education. He published an autobiography and a weekly abolitionist newspaper.

Problem-Solution

> ## MAIN IDEA
> Soil needs proper drainage for air to flow and facilitate plant growth.

> ## PROBLEM/S
> Soil becomes water-logged as the land becomes older and has more vegetable matter in it. Breaking-plows pulled by horses make the problem worse.

> ## SOLUTION/S
> Drains, particularly underdrains, can remove excess water.

Practice Exercise
1. a
2. b
3. a
4. b
5. a
6. d

LESSON 9
Exercise 1

COMPARISON (1)	SIMILE SIGN	COMPARISON (2)	ASPECT OF COMPARISON
Amanda	as	Her pet hamster	Anxious behavior
Dennis	like	Tick	Clinginess
Kerwin	like	Snail	Slowness
The man	as	Lion	Bravery
Angelo	like	Beetroot	Red

Exercise 2

COMPARISON (1)	COMPARISON (2)	ASPECT OF COMPARISON
Paul	Night owl	Being active at night
Clouds	Balls of cotton	White and fluffy
Anger	Volcano	Explosiveness
Katherine	Potato	Immobility
Books	Key	Used to unlock things

Exercise 3
1. a
2. "A host, of golden daffodils...Fluttering and dancing in the breeze."
3. Nature is being personified in the passage as it "could pity and be kind."

Exercise 4
1. c
2. c
3. d

Practice Exercises
Poem
1. a
2. c
3. b

Passage
1. a
2. b
3. d
4. b
5. d

LESSON 10
Practice Exercises

Passage 1	Passage 2
1. d	1. a
2. c	2. a

LESSON 11
Practice Exercise

Passage 1	Passage 2
1. d	3. a
2. b	4. c

5.

FACTS	OPINIONS
"If a pirate broke one of the many rules which governed the particular band to which he belonged, he was marooned…" "A suitable place was chosen (generally some desert isle as far removed as possible from the pathway of commerce), and the condemned man was rowed from the ship to the beach." "the largest number of pirate captains were Englishmen"	"The process of marooning was as simple as terrible." "leaving the poor wretch alone to rave away his life in madness, or to sit sunken in his gloomy despair till death mercifully" "the Englishman did the boldest and wickedest deeds"

LESSON 12
Practice Exercises
1. a
2. a
3. a
4. c
5. No, it is not a credible source as the writer is subjective and gives his opinions on what he observes in Brazil. He does not back up his claims with statistics and references.

ANSWER KEYS

PRACTICE TEST I

	PART A	PART B		PART A	PART B		PART A	PART B		PART A	PART B
1	b	c	11	c		21	a	c	31	c	
2	a		12	a		22	c		32	a	
3	d		13	c		23	b		33	b	
4	c	a	14	d		24	d		34	d	
5	d		15	a		25	b		35	c	a
6	a		16	b		26	b	d	36	d	
7	b		17	a	c	27	a		37	c	
8	a		18	b	d	28	c		38	c	
9	a		19	a		29	d		39	a	
10	c		20	d		30	c		40	b	a

PRACTICE TEST II

	PART A	PART B		PART A	PART B		PART A	PART B		PART A	PART B
1	c		11	c		21	b		31	d	
2	b		12	a		22	c		32	b	
3	b		13	b		23	a	c	33	b	c
4	a		14	d		24	a		34	a	
5	c		15	c	b	25	d		35	d	a
6	a	b	16	a		26	d	b	36	a	
7	b	d	17	a	c	27	a		37	c	
8	a		18	d		28	b		38	b	
9	d		19	b		29	c		39	d	
10	c		20	d		30	a		40	a	

ABOUT COACHING FOR BETTER LEARNING, LLC

CBL helps develop systems that increase performance and save time, resources and energy.

If you identify typos and errors in the text, please let us know at teamcbl@coachingforbetterlearning.com. We promise to fix them and send you a free copy of the updated textbook to thank you.